# Start Your Own
# Regional Gift Basket Business

## A Home-Based Business With National Customers

by Doris L. Miller

Limit of Liability / Disclaimer of Warranty:
The publisher and the author make no representation or warranty of the contents of this work as to the fitness for a particular purpose. The information, advice or suggestions contained within this book may not be appropriate for every situation. The publisher and author are not engaged in rendering legal, accounting, insurance or other professional services and strongly advises you to seek qualified professional services for your particular needs and situation.

Published in the United States by
Under The Shade Tree, LLC - Series B
PO Box 1071, Kaufman, Texas 75142


ISBN 978-0-9860501-1-4
Paperback Version
First Edition 2013

Library of Congress Control Number: 2013953618

Also available in E-Book Format
ISBN 978-0-9860501-0-7


Photographs courtesy of the author.

Business & Economics / Entrepreneurship          BUS025000
Business & Economics / Home-Based Businesses     BUS080000
Business & Economics / Small Business            BUS060000
Crafts & Hobbies / Baskets                       CRA002000

# Table Of Contents

# Introduction

In 2002 I created Lone Star Gift Baskets, a Texas gift basket company in Kaufman, Texas.

The company was started with only an idea. I didn't know how to make a basket, where to buy products, how to create a webpage or even market on the internet. All I wanted to do was give my customers great products and even better customer service.

Some would say I figured it out because on December 3, 2004 we were recognized by the Wall Street Journal as one of the 5 best regional basket companies in the USA. The Wall Street Journal didn't know the company consisted of only one individual at the time.

It is my goal in this book to share what I learned, things that worked and things that didn't, and what I discovered along the way. What worked for us may not work for you. By sharing my experiences I hope to make your journey a little easier and your job more enjoyable!

This book is not a design book or a basket idea book. You can find several quality "how-to" free videos on creating and wrapping themed baskets on the internet and on YouTube.com.

This book is intended to guide you as you create your own regional gift basket business. The book will help you find regional specific products, give you ideas on how to promote your company and everyday business ideas and personal experience items that may be helpful. I express my personal opinion about certain things along the way and others may (and probably will) disagree with me. In the book I tell a few stories - sometimes amusing and sometimes costly. I present this information so you will have a different perspective to draw from for your own business.

A regional gift basket business is a national business, not just a local one. Since the best way of attracting national customers is by using the internet, I have included information to help you create your website and to market your business using this valuable tool. Numerous free or low cost options and resources are presented throughout the text.

Make notes along the way and apply those things which will work for you and discard the rest. You are the ultimate decision maker and this is as it should be!

I wish you the best of luck with your new venture and lots of happy hours! There is joy and pride in helping your customers send a special, one of a kind gift, and sharing the tastes of your region or state with others. God Bless you with your ventures, now and in the future.

* * * * * *

Disclaimer - This book presents ideas and things that worked for me. Your particular situation may be different. There are no guarantees in the life of a new business. As I share my ideas with you, I am in no way guaranteeing your success. Your success will come through your own efforts and hard work.

The information presented should not be substituted for professional legal, tax or financial advice. I am not an accountant, insurance agent or a licensed attorney and the opinions expressed may not be appropriate for you. Always seek qualified council in business and money matters in your local area. The advice from a licensed professional will be worth your peace of mind knowing that you are doing everything within the laws of your city and state. These professionals can help avoid future headaches and possibly save you money. Ask for referrals in finding the professionals you need but please seek qualified council.

Trademarks listed in this book belong to their respective owners. Any product, company, website or service listed in this book has been provided for informational purposes only and does not constitute an endorsement of the company or their products. A decision to use these products, companies, websites or services is your own and should be made for your particular situation.

We assume no liability for a decision on your part to use any idea presented or to use any company, service or product listed in this book.

Please feel free to contact me with questions, suggestions or reference updates.

Now that we have that out of the way.....let's get started!

# Chapter 1
# Regional Gift Baskets

Gift baskets are wonderful since they have such a wide assortment of goodies and gifts. Unlike a single gift or flower arrangement, a gift basket is a collection of items, perhaps four to twenty different items, and a virtual treasure chest of goodies.

The regional gift basket sends the taste and flavor of a particular area with all of the surprises of a gift basket. Regional gift baskets have national appeal expanding your marketing area to all of America and not just your local customers.

Great for that special someone in boot camp, in school or away on business for months, regional gift baskets give them food from home, something "very familiar." Usually a very welcome gift!

What about new people moving to the area? A regional gift basket gives them a taste of what to expect when they move.

Regional gift baskets are great to say "thank you" to someone out of state that you stayed with over the holidays.

Gourmet food is always appreciated and can be the right gift for someone who is sick or who is feeling a little down.

Regional gift baskets are very much in demand. Sharing the flavor of your state or area with your brand of regional gift baskets, will be your marketing objective. You will be the creator of a particular regional collection making people happy - what a great feeling! If you were a retail clerk selling flower arrangements or single gifts, well, the feeling is just not the same!

1

The business is so enjoyable. You will talk to so many great people from all over the country. They will ask your advice on what to send and you can brag a little on how great your products are and help them send something really special.

Then there are the humorous customers trying to pull a prank and need your help. These individuals send their gifts with a card saying "From: George & Laura" or not signing it at all with instructions for you not to tell! Boy that drives them nuts! If you are a people person and enjoy chatting with a lot of different people, this is a great business for you. You can't help but make the business personal - it is so contagious!

Start planning your business only after you have determined that you can operate your home business where you live and if you have the space, time, money and support you will need. It will be much better if this business can involve the family, or at least have family support and understanding, instead of being something you have to do alone in addition to your other duties.

There will be long hours, hopefully, and the business will tend to bleed over into home and family time. You will try not to let this happen but the business telephone rings and you feel compelled to answer it. It is someone on the other coast, in a time zone where it is still 3:00 PM, and they want to place an order. Of course you take the call, and chat, and give them an estimate, and then supper is thirty minutes late or it's cold.

Such is the life of those who work at home. Make sure you and the family understand what this new business of yours could entail and try to get everyone involved. Help around the house sometimes is more appreciated than actually having help making baskets or talking to customers.

Developing your baskets and your business will take a week or two. I know you want to start making baskets but planning and research before you start is essential and can make the difference in how well your business will do in the future. Your due diligence and patience and will be well worth the effort and the wait.

# 1. The Planning Stage

Start with an internet search for regional basket companies in your state. By putting in "your state" "gift basket" - Texas gift basket, for example - in the search bar, you should find some of the most popular companies. Also, visit your state's section of the following basket directory sites:

Gift Basket Network - www.giftbasketnetwork.com
Gift Basket Superstore - www.gift-basket-superstore.com
Seek Gift Baskets - www.seekgiftbaskets.com


Take notes as you visit the different sites. Pick six or seven companies that really impress you when you visit. Use a separate sheet for each company. Put their name, web address and phone number across the top. As you go through their site, make notes on what you like and don't like.

1) What products do they carry? Which ones will you want in your baskets? If everyone seems to be carrying salsa or pecans, you probably should also. Make notes of the brands they carry so you can contact the manufacturer later.

2) What kinds of containers are they using for their baskets? The common gift boxes or actual baskets? Woven baskets from China or are they using a state shaped basket or tray?

3) Do they sell individual products in gift boxes or do they just do gift baskets?

4) What are their price ranges? The least expensive basket and the most expensive.

5) Which credit cards do they take? Only MasterCard and Visa or do they offer American Express, Discover, etc.?

6) Do they have a large selection or only 1 - 2 baskets? Does every basket seem to contain the same products?

7) Are the actual products small and mostly wrapping and packaging?

8) How do they deliver their baskets? Do they only use USPS or do they offer UPS and Fedex? Do they ship out the same day or next day? Do they hand deliver or offer same day delivery? Do their delivery times seem reasonable?

9) How do they charge for delivery? Do they use the shipping company's calculators or do they have a graduated scale by purchase price? If they use a graduated scale write it down.

10) Do you like the website? Is it professional and easy to navigate? Make notes of what you like, such as the menu buttons on the top or would you prefer them on the side?

11) Try putting something in the shopping cart and then going to checkout. Is the process easy or confusing? Is it one page or several? Does the shipping and tax amounts show before you complete your purchase?

12) Check out their "About Us" page. Does it read like a cold corporate review or is it more personal and customer oriented?

13) If there is something that is not clear, call them. Ask the questions that a customer would ask and try not to be obvious. If you want to know about their shipping, creating custom baskets or substituting one product for another, call and see what they say.

14) Are all of their products made in your state or region?

15) If you call, make a note about how they answer the phone. Are they pleasant and want to help or are they rude? Do they know their products? Did they offer solutions and suggestions?

You will start to size up your competition as you get the answers and concentrate on being different from all of the rest. Is there something that you can do that is not being done now? Is there something that is being done but not very well? Can you do better? Make a list of what you would do or things you would change.

Write down why your customers would care about the things you want to change. How will it benefit your customers? Why would customers choose to do business with you? Will you offer products they can't get anywhere else? Will your products be better quality or perhaps in a larger size? Can you make customers feel really special and appreciated when you take their order? Think about why a customer would want to choose you over XYZ down the road.

I want to stress that you should never copy someone else's website or business model. Your goal is to be different from the competition - something really special. You will use the answers to your questions to develop your baskets and your website. If, for instance, you would like to put your navigation buttons at the top of your website like XYZ, that is alright, but don't make your whole website look like theirs with the same colors, wording and photo locations. Websites are covered by copyright laws and you should never copy someone else's creation.

# 2. Your Special Products

In your planning stage, you discovered what everyone else is selling or maybe you discovered something that was missing. Sometimes what you don't see is as important as what you do.

Perhaps these companies have carried a particular product that you are interested in and their customers did not like it. Don't reinvent the wheel. Call and ask if they have XYZ product, knowing full well they don't, and you may get lucky. The salesperson may say, "we did carry that item, but we couldn't sell it" or "we tried that product but it was always stale." Now you know not to carry this product and you didn't have to find out the hard way.

By now you should be developing an idea about your own regional gift baskets and what you want in them. You will want some of the more common smaller products that everyone seems to carry - jelly beans, popcorn, nuts, snack mixes and chocolate (messy if you live or ship to the hotter parts of the country). Your larger items should be the more expensive, gourmet type products that really highlight your region or your state. Think about your area and the foods that set it apart and make a preliminary list.

The next step is to see what is available to you and where to locate your products. Chapter 3 - Locating Your Products, will help you to locate manufacturing companies in your area with products for your specific state or region. Most have their websites listed with the Department of Agricultures and this will make it easy to find products you are interested in. Call or e-mail them for catalogs. Most of the companies will be happy to talk to you, give you wholesale prices, delivery times and may offer you free sample products.

While your emphasis may be on food type items, be sure to check out the other association websites. For example, the leather association will have members manufacturing coasters and key fobs that would be great for cattle producing states like Texas, Wyoming, Montana, etc. For states that produce granite and marble, check out the manufacturers of small paperweights with the state flag or seal on the top.

When the catalogs and the samples start arriving, what you thought you were going to carry may change. You will find products that no one else is carrying and perhaps develop a specialty all your own.

When we think of regional gift baskets, we automatically think of gourmet food but that may not be the case once you start your research. You may decide to specialize in a specific type basket -

goody baskets for our furry friends, bath type items, potpourri and candles or perhaps baby care items, all made in your region, of course. Some companies offer the gourmet foods but they specialize in only chocolate items, nuts and treats or in organic or gluten free foods.

Your particular regional gift basket will start to develop once you see what others carry, what they don't offer and the hundreds of other products available to you. Once you see all of your options, your specialty may be something that you have never thought about. Keep an open mind to new ideas as they present themselves in this discovery stage.

# 3. Being Different

You will need a signature for your company, something that will set you apart from all the rest. Your mission statement will be an important part of your signature. You should express how you are different and make it a promise to your customers.

I started in business quite by accident trying to find a cup actually made in Texas. Three problems soon became evident in the sites that I visited and my correction to these three things later became the company's mission statement and our promise to our customers:

1) We would only sell items actually made in Texas, including our baskets.

2) Our products would be substantial in size - not tiny sample sizes. And finally,

3) We pledged to state exactly what was in our baskets and the sizes.

On our website and in all of our advertising, these three things were highlighted to set us apart. In your research you found things that you want to do differently. State your promise to your customers and use this promise as your signature.

Smaller things can set you apart, such as a color. Think about Home Depot orange or Lowes blue - even their tools are their respective color!

Your signature color can be the actual color of every basket you send out or just a ribbon added around the top of your baskets. Use your signature color as the back drop for your products in every photo to unify your website.

Since you are specializing in regional baskets, perhaps your colors should correspond with your state's flag colors. Our Texas flag is red, white and blue and these were our colors. Our advertising used blue ink on white paper, the text on our website was blue, the backdrop behind our baskets in photos was royal blue and the raffia ribbons on each of our baskets were one each of red, white and blue.

Your signature may be a single item you add to each and every basket. An example would be a silk flower representing your state flower, like a bluebonnet for Texas. A photo postcard from your area with a little local history would be inexpensive and informative. A small souvenir item from your local area could be used. For instance, Grand Saline, Texas has a historic salt mine and at the museum they sell a one inch cube of salt along with information about the mine and the area for about a dollar. If your area or region has something like this, add it to each of your baskets as your signature.

A signature phrase is also important. Something to express your business in a few words. Don't be silly or cute - that is not the impression you want to make with a multi-million dollar customer! Think about what you offer and the service you provide: "If it's not Made In Texas, it's not in our baskets" or plainly stated "Authentic Texas Gift Baskets Made In The USA." Use your signature phrase on everything - your website, business cards, brochures and on any advertising you send out.

# 4. Basket Rules For Regional Baskets

Rule 1 - Treat people with respect, love what you do and only give your customers great products and wonderful customer service. If you do these things your competition will not be a problem. This is true even if your products cost more.

Rule 2 - Regional gift baskets should carry only products made in your actual area or state. Insist that your products be made in your area, or don't offer them. More Americans are trying to only buy products made in the USA and this attitude is perfect for your new regional business.

Rule 3 - Never mix food and smells. Never add scented items like candles or potpourri to a food basket. The scents will infiltrate the food through the plastic packaging and the soup, candy or chili, etc., will taste horrible. Scented items should not even be in the same room where your food is stored. This includes air fresheners, hair spray, perfume, etc., or anything that you spray or that emits a smell of any kind.

# 5. Developing Your Baskets

Now that you have an idea of what products you want to carry, and where to get them, you will need to develop your basket combinations. This is fun because it doesn't cost anything.

At the kitchen table, or in the middle of the floor, lay out a large piece of paper or clean newsprint. Divide the paper in sections by drawing lines or by folding side to side and top to bottom. The sections don't have to be exact, just make several large boxes.

Start in the first section writing down items for your first basket. Try to add items that coordinate well with each other. Some Texas examples would be:

Chili for the main course, cornbread and candied jalapenos would be good additions. Now add a desert - peach cobbler or a canned cake. Throw in a package of pecans for nibbling and a Texas trivia book for after dinner reading.

Your second basket may be for the guys that cook on the grill. A bottle of liquid marinade, maybe a couple of seasoning rubs and steak sauce, throw in a couple of pecan pralines for snacking as they cook and you have a basic grilling basket.

Your third basket may be all sweets. Pecans, pralines, chocolate tamales, a canned cake and a jar of blackberry cobbler.

As you create your combinations, think about a special person that you want to create a basket for, perhaps an avid gardener. The container might be a plastic planter or pot filled with gloves, seeds for your area, some tools, sunblock lotion and maybe a flavored herb tea and a tea cup or mug.

Depending on where you live, and the climate, the basket combinations that you put together will be totally different from the ones on the other coast, or two states North. When you think of Maine you think of fishing, lobsters & cold weather. When you think of Florida you think of beaches, sun and fun. When you think of Texas you think of chili, barbeque and cowboys on the range.

Basket combinations also depend on the season. Soup baskets are great for the winter months and grilling items are almost mandatory for the summer. Snack baskets and sweets are great all year long.

Use your own list of native items that you want to carry and coordinate a dozen or so combinations. As you look at your combinations, think about size and weight. The larger and heavier the basket, the harder it is to handle. A large basket costs more to ship and has a greater chance of getting damaged in shipping. This doesn't mean you shouldn't do a large gift basket. Our largest basket weighed 23 pounds and shipped in a 24 X 18 X 9 inch box. Even though we didn't have a problem shipping these Texas Giants, after a while my arm had a problem!

When you actually assemble your goodies for the basket, you may find that you have too many glass items or things that don't fit right. You may need to increase the size of the container if you want to keep the combination of items you have assembled. We will work on finalizing your baskets later on.

Play with your product list and move items around in the squares. After you have several combinations, use different colored highlighters, one color for each product, to see how many of your combinations have the same products. This color coding makes it very easy to see duplications.

You may find that most of your baskets have pralines, for example. Small items that are individually packages and easily obtained, are ok to have in multiple baskets. If you find that you have chili in every basket, rethink your basket combinations. Try to make combinations without being too repetitive with your products and each should be distinctly different. One advantage to having the same items in multiple baskets is your inventory item list is shorter. The disadvantage is when you run out of this product it effects more than one basket.

# 6. Naming Your Baskets

In each of your squares you have assembled a collection of items that are somehow related and their basket names should reflect this association. Think about your region or your state when you give each of your baskets their name.

If I were to name the baskets we did earlier and give them Texas names, they might sound like this: Texas Chuckwagon Cooking Basket, Texas Grilling Basket, Texas Sweet Treats Basket and the last may be the Texas Gardening Delight Basket.

Perhaps use the nick name of your state in your names: the Lone Star Chuckwagon Cooking Basket, the Lone Star Grilling Basket, the Lone Star Sweet Treats Basket and the Lone Star Gardening Delight Basket.

Other appropriate Texas names might be the Cowgirl Basket, Home On The Range Basket, Millionaires Basket, Dallas' Best Basket, Texas Pecan Basket, Salsa Party Basket, Good Morning Texas Basket, Texas Snacking Basket. You get the idea.

One added advantage of using the name of your state in the title of your baskets, it gives the search engines another way of finding your particular regional baskets. When someone does a search for Texas gift baskets and Google finds the words "Texas" and "Basket," in all four of the baskets above, the search results will be more in your favor, which is a great thing.

# 7. Describing Your Baskets

Make someone reading the basket descriptions on your website really want one! Make it sound like it is the best thing around. Paint them a picture.

Using the gardening basket that we created earlier, its description may sound like this: "The Gardener's Delight Basket has everything for your gardening enjoyment! Our colorful container would be lovely sitting on the patio or in your yard.

We have included some local wildflower seeds to plant and watch grow. A tending fork tool will help keep the weeds at bay. Protect your hands with our special cloth gloves and don't forget to wear your sunblock that we have included! When the day is done, come in and relax with a cup of flavored tea in your new tea cup, handmade by Cyndi the potter from Yourtown."

Don't just list items in your baskets, describe the scene, make it come alive. Tell them what they will be doing with all of the goodies in the basket. Make the descriptions pop!

# 8. Baskets And Containers

Since you are specializing in regional gift baskets, your containers should actually be made in your state. These can be the shape of your state or something other than a basket - a miniature lobster basket for those in Maine or a Sand Castle bucket and scoop for those on the coast. What about a red wagon for those in Illinois or a miniature bushel basket for the regions that grows so much of our wheat and corn?

You will start looking at everything as a container - vases, wagons, hats, buckets, bowls, planter pots, mugs - almost anything can be used.

Custom boxes or trays with handles can be made for you at a local box company. Set up a meeting to see what is available and how they can help you decide what would work best. These can be imprinted with your name and logo but you will be asked to commit to a large quantity to keep the individual cost down. Even if you can't afford it now, set up the meeting and get some ideas for later.

If you sell individual products, or sets of products, a strong box with an attached lid would speed up your shipping and would give your customers another way of purchasing your items. Sometimes a gift basket with all of the frills doesn't fit your customer's needs - they are after the goodies and not the foo-foo! The shipping supply company where you buy your boxes and bubble wrap can get inserts of molded foam or soft cushioning material made for your custom boxes. After you decide on the size of the box and what you will be shipping, ask for an insert quote. This is a more costly option but it looks very professional and speeds up your order processing.

Keep at least three sizes of baskets or other containers in stock. Some corporate customers will want the biggest basket you have while someone sending a personal basket may opt for a less expensive basket. Be sure to have a couple of each on hand. Nested baskets bought in sets are great but I would recommend that you buy baskets individually. When you buy in groups you tend to have a lot of one size left over that no one seems to want. After a while you will find the price points of your particular customers and know more about the sizes to carry.

Stay with neutral colors - I would always use the natural basket with a natural ribbon around the top. The vendor can get you other colors for special occasions like bright orange for a University of Texas football basket or a maroon color for Texas A&M. Your local basket maker should have a selection for the section of the country that you are in. The exception to this is if you make the basket color a signature of your company - all blue baskets for instance. One more way of setting you apart from the competition.

# Chapter 2
# Basket Business Basics

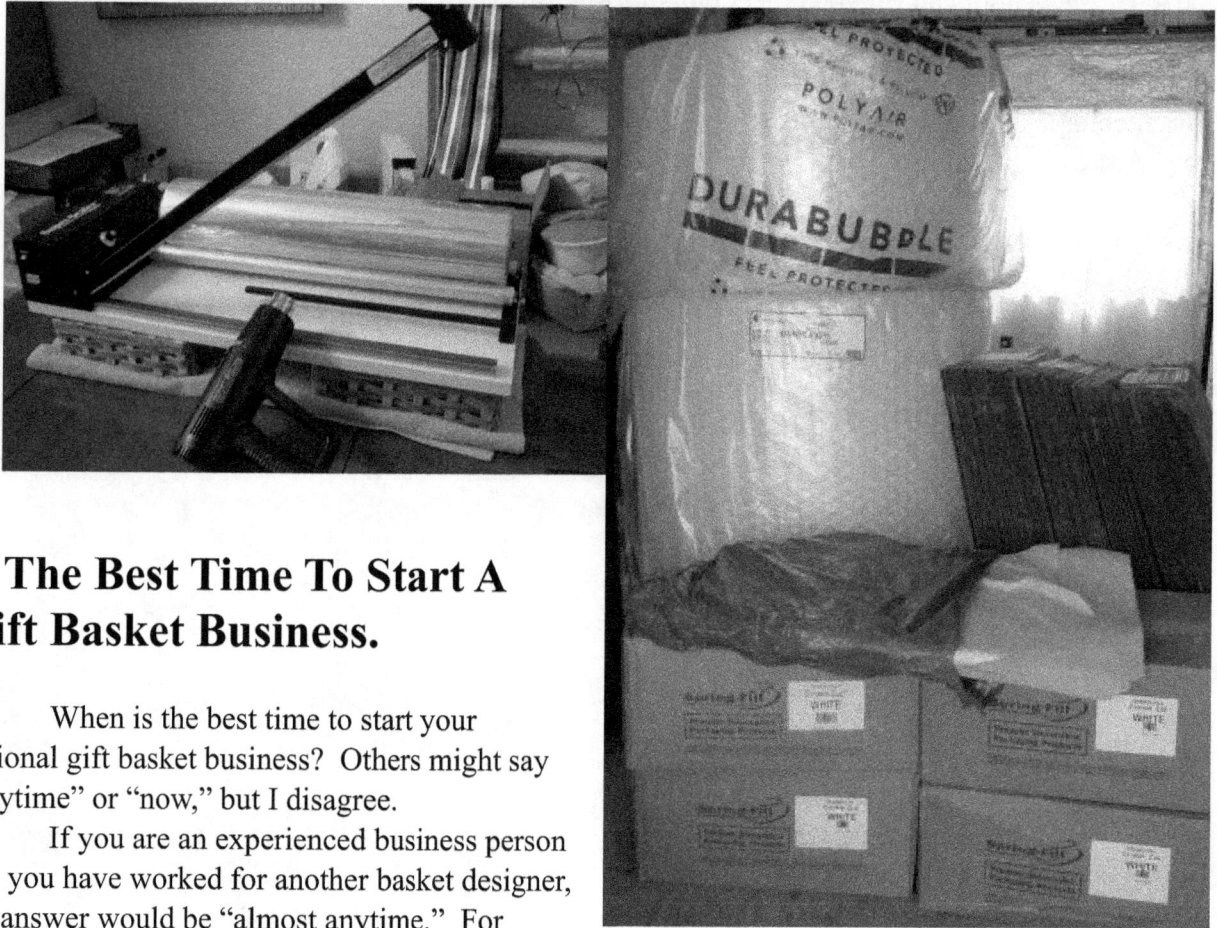

## 1. The Best Time To Start A Gift Basket Business.

When is the best time to start your regional gift basket business? Others might say "anytime" or "now," but I disagree.

If you are an experienced business person and you have worked for another basket designer, the answer would be "almost anytime." For someone who knows nothing about the business, the first part of the year would be the best time.

If you are unexperienced, like I was, you need to have time to work out your products, your gift wrapping techniques, your work schedule and even your business forms and office practices.

The early part of the year is much slower than around Christmas and this will allow you to develop your basket and business skills. This is very important before you try to tackle a full Christmas season. Christmastime will be your busiest season so you should feel confident in your abilities prior to being presented with a huge rush of customers. This is not a time for amateurs if you want to stay in business with your reputation intact. My advice would be to start early in the year, or at least several months before December, and develop your skills.

# 2. What Do I Need To Start This Venture?

This is kind of an open question. I had estimated that it would take $2500 for my startup costs. I did not have a business plan that I presented to a lender because I started small and added items as I went instead of incurring an initial loan or credit card bill. It took me about six months before I actually had everything that I wanted for the business, adding items as I sold baskets and made a little money. The computer and shelving I had and I added supplies, products and tools as I could. All of my profits went right back into the business at first.

Depending on whether you are starting this as an internet only business or a small home-based business serving the local area, your costs will vary. You may be able to find someone going out of business to purchase things like the sealer and turntable. Craig's List (www.craigslist.com) is a great place to find business items, tables and file cabinets.

Check locally for a company that will sell you the boxes, tape, bubble wrap and clean newsprint. Ask if they keep the boxes and supplies you need in their warehouse. If they have to order these, it could take a couple of extra days, so ask if they would stock extras for you until you need them. This would be really handy during the holiday rush. These companies can sell you larger quantities at much better prices compared to buying single items at an office supply or discount house.

The following list of items is pretty complete to run the business, but use your situation and budget to guide your buying decisions. You may not need, or want, everything on this list. Use this as a check list and add your local prices for your chosen items. The prices listed were correct as of publication:

_____DBA / LLC / Incorporation Filing and Registration Fees

40.00  Table - approx. 2 X 6 foot - A laminated countertop works great with legs added.

32.90  Turntable

325.00  24 inch Sealer - SS24D with 100 feet of 100 gauge Food Grade PVC & Heat Gun

59.00  18 inch X 500 feet - 100 gauge Food Grade PVC - Centerfold shrink wrap

37.90  20inch X 250 feet - 100 gauge Food Grade PVC - Tube shrink wrap

36.00  Glue Dots - 1000 - 1/2 inch High Tack / High Profile

52.50  Raffia or pearl - 3 different colors - 500 yards each @ 17.50

25.80  Gold Gift Cards - 250 - fold over - self sticking - appropriate for all occasions

_____  Imprinted Company Labels

22.50  Crinkle Cut Basket Shreds - 10# White

30.50  Clean Newsprint - 24 X 36 inch - 30 pounds - about 400 sheets

22.75  Desktop 2 inch tape dispenser with 3 inch core

_____ Handheld 2 inch tape dispenser with 3 inch core

_____ Scale - needs to be able to weigh 25 pounds or more.

_____ 1/2 inch Heavy Duty Bubble Wrap - The lighter version does not work well for glass items. 4 foot rolls - 250 feet long, perfed every 12 inches.  These 4 foot rolls can be cut into 2 - 24 inch rolls or 3 - 16 inch rolls to fit your needs.

_____ Boxes - usually come in straps of 15 - 25 each.

_____ 2 inch Heavy Shipping Tape - approx. $3.00 per roll - generally comes in a 36 roll case.

_____ Hosting for your website - most companies will include your annual Domain name registration fee in the cost of hosting.

_____ Merchant account to receive payment

_____ Digital Camera

_____ Baskets or Containers / Products and Inventory of your choice.  Start with a list of the items that you will need to make your particular style of baskets, using your manufacturer catalogs and price sheets.

# 3. Additional Business Items

Desk Planner - Daily Planner - Auto Mileage Log - A large desk planner is a great tool to let you see a whole month at a time.  You can put deadlines, order dates and expected delivery dates clearly in view and find things quickly at a glance.

A daily planner is used to record any details, how many packages went out in a day, any special happening during the day and anything else that you may need to refer to in the future.

A small mileage log book and pen should be kept in your vehicle and any trips you make for the business recorded.  Record the date, the odometer or trip counter reading before and after your trip, where you went and for what reason.  A brief description is extremely important to support your mileage use and deduction on your income tax.  The notation should be something like this: 8/1/2013 - 1400/ 1410 - 10 miles Dallas - Post office & office supply store.

Brochures - If you have a computer and a good printer, create a few brochures to keep on hand.  For a large mail out I would recommend a professional printing.  Appearance matters with your corporate customers.   I used very few brochures, referring our customers to our website instead.  The website should contain the most current product information and basket combinations.

Business Cards - Start out with a 1000 good quality cards and give these away to everyone that you meet.  A 1000 only costs a few dollars more than 500.  A good quality card is important - don't scrimp! Plain cards or unprofessionally printed ones get thrown away. Tuck one or two cards in every basket just under the products.  Add a card in each invoice or receipt you mail.

Advertising Post Cards - Can be mailed, put into the baskets or included in the envelope with your custom order invoices. We used 4 X 6 four color postcards printed with a photo of our largest basket on the front and our contact and product info in black ink on the reverse side. On the color photograph there was a small white "cloud" behind our name, slogan and website address to highlight the information.

Satisfaction Post Cards - Include these in your baskets requesting information from the individuals that receive your baskets. Questions like: Did the basket arrive in good condition? What did you think of the overall basket? What was your favorite item? Was there anything in the basket that you did not like? Taylor the questions to fit your needs and what you would like to know from those receiving your baskets.

These can be printed in black ink with your return address on one side. Put the order number on the card so you will know which order it belongs.

Reorder Stickers - When you purchase your products from the manufacturer, your customers see where the products are made. Have some stickers printed with "Reorder From 'your company'." Include your name, telephone number and website and attach these to your products in a place that does not interfere with any of the important information from the manufacturer. The lid is often a good location. When the bottle or jar is empty, your customers can call to reorder if they can easily find your name and contact information.

Glue Dots - 1/2 inch high, medium to high stickiness - these are great! They provide a cushion between your products (not quite enough between 2 glass jars, though) and they come off without destroying your packaging. The heavier the stickiness, the more the chance of part of the packaging being damaged.

Some designers use glue guns but I never did. The excess glue "strings" get messy, the hot glue can damage the food packaging and can burn you, and unlike the glue dots the hot glue does not provide a cushion between products.

Scale - Choose one able to weigh 25 pounds or more. The scale should have a large surface for your boxes and an easy to read display.

Boxes - Use only new, good quality, corrugated boxes. They should be able to support your products and withstand the punishment from the shipping companies. Try to get your box selection down to only 3 or 4 sizes. You can have 20 or 30 basket variations but you will only have to keep a couple of box sizes on hand. This simplifies ordering and usually your supplier can keep a few straps (sets of 15 - 25) on hand for your busy times. Check with the box company and ask about their busy time of the year. My supplier was slow during the holidays so this worked out great for both of us. If your supplier is busy during the holidays, be sure to have them hold an extra supply for you in their warehouse.

Tape and Dispensers - Don't get the cheapest, lightest tape available - you will waste as much as you use! Get a stronger tape, one that doesn't backlash when you are closing a box. If you are not sure what to ask for, go to the shipping supply company and ask to see their selection and actually use the tape. They will be glad to help since you will be buying this in a case lot. Trust me when I tell you 36 rolls of crummy tape will seem to last forever! A clear tape is best because you can use this for repairing tiny holes in your wrap if necessary. The shipping tape is usually 2 inches wide with a 3 inch core. A hand held dispenser works well for closing boxes and I also recommend a table top dispenser for this same size tape. These are weighted and are great to keep on your wrapping table for repairs, etc.

Bubble Wrap - If you are sending heavy baskets with lots of glass items, I recommend you use 1/2 inch heavy weight bubble. There is also a 1/2 inch light duty, but this pops too easily and you are depending on the bubble to protect your products. There seems to be very little cost difference between the light and heavy duty bubble. Don't scrimp on the bubble wrap, even if the heavy version costs more. Popped bubble = broken products = lost products & lost profit = upset customers.

Peanuts - I did not purchase these because of the cost and the necessary storage space but I kept and reused the peanuts that came with my supplies along with clean newsprint. You can purchase peanuts that are biodegradable and static free. There is a hopper that attaches to the ceiling to get your peanuts off the floor if you want to use this method.

Air Cushion Machine - Inflatable air pillows or quilted bubble sheets. These are fairly new and come deflated in rolls with perfs after each pillow. The machine that inflates and seals the pillows takes up only a small area and could be an option to save space. Shop around for the best prices since these are expensive. Make sure the pillows will be large enough to protect your baskets before purchasing. I chose not to use this option because of the cost and the 6 inch pillows were not large enough to protect our baskets.

Clean Newsprint - Comes flat in packages of about 400 - 800 sheets, approximately 24 X 36 inches and weighs about 50 pounds. You can find different sizes and weights. I suggest using only clean, unprinted newsprint so you don't get printers ink all over your beautiful package. The clean newsprint also gives a professional appearance instead of a "make do" operation.

Butcher Paper - Comes in rolls about 18 inches X 1100 ft and weighs about 30 pounds. You can purchase a table top holder/cutter for your rolls that makes handling much easier. Heavier than newsprint, this paper is good for packing but is a little harder to handle.

Ribbon - Raffia - pull bows - curling ribbon - ribbon. I used pull bows at first. They take up very little space and make up quickly when needed. Later we switched to red, white and blue ribbon and raffia.

If you want to make your own custom bows, check out Offray Ribbon (www.offray.com) or Lyon Ribbon (www.lyonribbon.com) for instructions on custom bow making.

Whatever type of ribbon or bow you decide to use, consider how you will have to package a gift for shipping to keep the bow from being crushed. This was also a factor when I decided to go to ribbon and raffia since there wasn't a fluffy bow to protect from damage.

Cello - Cello comes in all sorts of gorgeous prints and needed widths. Cello makes a beautiful basket but I would suggest only using it for lighter, local, hand delivered baskets. Anything that needs to be boxed and shipped should be shrink wrapped to stabilize the products and prevent damage and breakage.

Tube Shrink Wrap - The tube wrap is handy to make your own gift bags. Cut off the length you need plus several inches. On one end tuck each side in a couple of inches and secure the sides with clips or clothes pins. Seal the end across these tucks and you have your own gift bag. Work on the length and how much to "tuck in" to perfect your bags for your particular use.

Gift Cards - A beautiful gold, silver or white card can be used for any occasion. Pick one that is folded with an adhesive strip on the back - just rip off the tape and position on your gift under the bow. The gold and silver work well for gifts that require a business like presentation.

Purchase Christmas and holiday gift cards in late December and January. Out of season items are usually 50% off, take up very little room and buying out of season saves you money.

Hang Tags - These can be made by you on the computer and cut with a pinking shear, folded once and a hole punched in one corner. If you print on a parchment type paper they look classy but not so executive as the gold gift card. These work well for someone sending a birthday greeting. You can insert the ends of the ribbon through the punched hole as you make your bow.

Imprinted Company Labels - I like the gold ovals with the print following the curve on the top and bottom with the website located across the center.

Attach one on the bottom of your basket if you are not using a stamp or brander. The downside to using these on the bottom of the basket is that they tend to come off easily.

When the basket is complete and wrapped, add another label on top. Unlike the basket itself, the labels don't want to come off of the shrink wrap. Wait until the basket is wrapped and the bow is attached prior to deciding where the sticker needs to go. Almost every time I put a sticker on a basket, prior to adding the raffia or the bow, the ribbon covered my label!

Shipping Stickers - "Fragile," "Protect from Freezing" or even a directional sticker "This Way Up" can be purchased if you feel the need. If you would like your company name on your boxes but can't afford the custom printed ones, consider a bumper sticker printed with your company information. Created with some thought, your information can appear several times on a single large bumper sticker and then cut apart. This would be a less expensive way to identity your product on the shipping boxes.

Self Inking Stamp - Can be used on the bottom of your baskets. Be sure the stamp gives all of the vital information - telephone number, website, etc. The stamp should identify you as a designer of baskets, not the manufacturer, and should not cover their information.

For example:

**Gift basket assembled by Yellow Cottage Gifts**
**www.yellowcottagegifts.com**
**555-555-5555**

Branding Iron - Costly but is a nice touch on solid bottom wooden tray type baskets. Rockler (www.Rockler.com) offers custom branding irons. Practice on a broken basket prior to actually using it on your good basket stock! You need to know just how long to leave it on the wood to make a crisp brand without having all of the letters run together like one big burnt blob. Not as easy to use as a rubber stamp or a label but a great look and is permanent. As with any heated tool, use extreme caution.

Freezer / Refrigerator - These are big ticket items that you may want to add as the business grows. Refrigeration will extend some products' shelf life and a separate freezer or refrigerator from your personal one will be a blessing. After all, who wants onion flavored pecans? Remember, smells transfer so keep this in mind when using your personal refrigerator.

Foo Foo - I love that word! Anything from greenery, ting-ting to silk flowers can be used to add a little interest and pizzazz to your basket. Your state's flower in a silk version would be a nice addition to your regional gift baskets and could be your signature touch for every basket.

Photo Portfolio - Keep a photo book of any special custom baskets you do. These photos can be used when you are on a sales call along with photos of your regular baskets. Put the digital photo ID number on the back of the photo so you can easily locate the original on your computer for reference or to e-mail to a new customer.

# 4. Licenses And Permits

Check with your state and local authorities for necessary licenses and permits. The following list will get you started but may not apply, or be complete, for your local area to operate a gift basket or home-based business. Do your homework prior to going into business or spending any money. You don't want to get all set up and find you can't operate your business!

## (a) Local Restrictions And City Codes

Call the city that you live in and find out if they allow home-based businesses. Some areas have Home Owners Associations (HOA) which enforce restrictions in addition to the city codes, so contact your HOA if you have one.

In most instances, unless you tell your neighbors what you are doing, no one will know or probably care. They may have an objection to the UPS truck coming to the house every day, but others get packages so why shouldn't you. Most of the objections to a home-based business is the increased traffic in an otherwise quiet area - think of a continuous garage sale. Since you will not have customers coming to the house and the business is a very quiet one, the HOA and the city shouldn't have a problem with a basket business in your home.

I can not stress enough, check prior to spending any money or planning any major changes to accommodate your new enterprise.

## (b) State Sales Taxes And Collection Permits

Once you are sure you can operate your new business as planned, contact your State's Comptroller to obtain an application to collect sales taxes. They will give you an outline of what you collect tax on and when you do not have to add the tax. Adhere to their policies and keep good records. They can request to see your sales records and ask how you arrived at the figure that you submitted at anytime. If you don't collect the sales taxes and an audit reveals you should have, you will be liable for the payment of the tax, not your customer. Depending on your sales you may only be required to pay once a year or your state may want a monthly accounting.

Having a virtual storefront, versus a brick and mortar store, may make a difference in the sales taxes you collect. Most of the time you collect sales taxes on products delivered within your state. If the product is delivered to a different state, the recipient is usually responsible for paying any tax due. In some states food is not taxable but in others your baskets will be considered gifts and fully taxable, including the shipping charges.

Ask questions of the State Comptroller's office until you completely understand every requirement and what they expect of you. Write down the name of the person you spoke with, the date and time, along with any other notes. Don't feel foolish asking questions. If you don't get it clarified before you start it could cost you dearly later. Ask questions until you are comfortable with what you are doing and what they expect. If you get different answers every time you call and ask the same question, ask to speak to a supervisor or even to an attorney in the comptroller's office. If referred to the attorney's office, get any ruling sent to you in letter form by mail or e-mail and file it with your important papers. You will need this letter to support your actions in the future should an audit be conducted.

### (c) Health Department License And Inspections

Items like jelly beans, pecans and nuts can be purchased in bulk a lot cheaper than pre-packaged, but the drawbacks might outweigh the price difference. By buying in bulk you need to have packaging, proper labels, an accurate scale, insurance to cover manufacturers product liability, a commercial kitchen with inspections and permits from your local health department. The added headache of one more permit and someone coming to inspect your kitchen, may be enough for you to go in another direction. Generally commercial kitchens are not allowed in residential areas - so there goes your home-based business.

You may want to avoid this all together. Check with your local health department but in most cases if you do not handle the actual food, you are not subject to a health inspection. Once again contact the health department in your area and ask questions.

Purchasing the individually packaged items was actually a time and money saver for me. Not only did I not want the added liability issues, I wanted everyone to see where the products were made throughout my state. The different company labels actually reinforced my philosophy and proved where in the state the products were made. You may want to start with prepackaged items and later explore your own commercial kitchen idea. Who knows, you may come up with your own product to promote to other basket companies!

Several companies will "private label" their products (print your company's name on the label - "Made for Gift Baskets of Maine") but check with your insurance company prior to doing this. Sometimes this shifts the manufacturer's product liability from them to you. This is one issue I never faced since I wanted everyone to know where in Texas our products were made. Since you are doing regional gift baskets this may be your feeling as well.

### (d) Personal ID Or EIN Number

If you are operating the business under a DBA you can use your personal Social Security number to get a sales tax number and open your bank account, but because of identity theft, the fewer people who have your Social Security number, the better.

Contact the IRS and get a personal identification number. You can apply online at www.irs.gov, by mail or fax, or by calling 800-829-4933. The IRS will tie your Social Security Number to the ID number and you will use this new number instead of your social security number in all of your business dealings.

If you have formed a LLC or Corporation, the IRS will issue an EIN in the name of the company.

### (e) Wine And Spirits

One item that many gift basket companies carry is some type of wine or spirits.

Alcohol is generally regulated by the state and a permit is required which is usually quite expensive. There is an added delivery expense since the basket must be signed for at the delivery point by a person over the age of 21. Another issue is the selection of the wines and maintaining them in a proper wine cooler. For personal reasons, along with the cost and regulations involved, I chose not to sell wine in our baskets. As your company grows, you might consider adding wine to your baskets.

### (f) Additional Education

Do you need a refresher course on how to use Word or a data base? Boost your confidence and your abilities with a little extra education. These online classes may prove helpful:

Lynda.com - www.lynda.com - 888-335-9632. An online classroom offering instruction in web design, e-commerce, online marketing, writing, business coaching and skills, accounting and bookkeeping, word processing, data base and spreadsheets.

They also offer classes on the use of Facebook, Twitter, Linkedin and YouTube for promoting your business.

Lynda.com offers a free 7 day trial to use any of their classes. A subscription is about $25 per month to take any or all of their classes. There are over 1800 video classes ranging from an hour to several hours long. A great, inexpensive way to learn new skills or brush up on skills you haven't used in a while.

ed2go - www.edtogo.com - This is online learning through a local college near you. They have all kinds of classes that usually last six weeks and cost about $100 each. These are continuing education type classes with interaction between students and professors.

Classes are offered in business, marketing, accounting, finance, writing and technology.

# 5. Naming Your Business

Spend plenty of time choosing your business name. Hopefully, you will have to live with your decision for a very long time and you will need a name prior to filing your legal papers and opening a bank account.

Choose a name that is not easily confused with your competition but one that clearly identifies what you do or where you are located. Many companies incorporate their state or region's name - Baskets from Tennessee or Lower Valley Baskets or a state's nickname like Lone Star Basket Creations in the state of Texas.

Your website domain name should match your business name, so try to keep it short for the convenience of yourself and your customers. A long name is harder to type, has a greater chance of spelling errors and you will get tired of typing it yourself.

Before choosing a name for the company, see if the matching domain name is available. You may want to change the company name slightly to be able to obtain a matching domain name. Most hosting companies who offer domain name registration will have a tool on their website to check name availability. If your choice is reserved, some sites will make recommendations for other similar names you might like.

Here are a couple of websites to use for your name search:

www.westhost.com
www.networksolutions.com
www.godaddy.com

## (a) Making Your Name Official

The legal form of your business will effect the amount of taxes you will pay, reporting forms, insurance issues such as liability coverage and policy costs. This is definitely an area to get professional advice at the start and a good CPA or business attorney can help. Your choice will effect your business for a very long time so seek qualified counsel.

### (i) An Assumed Name Or DBA

Check your state's laws, but in Texas we have 254 counties and when a company is operated under an assumed name or DBA (Doing Business As), there could conceivably be 254 companies within the State using the same name - one per county. Often companies will file DBA's in surrounding counties just to protect their territory.

Usually this form can be completed and filed in the County Clerk's office at the courthouse requiring a nominal fee to record the document. This form lets the public know that you intend on doing business in that particular county, using a name other than your own. In Texas this filing reserves your name in the county that it is filed for 10 years. You may need several certified copies of this document for use in obtaining insurance, opening a bank account, etc.

### (ii) Incorporate Your New Business

Filing a DBA does not necessarily prevent someone from incorporating a business in your state using your company's name. You will spend a lot of time cultivating the company's name and product reputation and to receive a 'cease and desist' order to discontinue using it would be devastating. If your name is unique, or you are worried about someone else using your company name, investigate a Limited Liability Company (LLC) or some other type of Incorporation.

Incorporation can give you certain personal liability protection that a DBA can't and the type of incorporation (there are more than one) will affect the way you report and pay your income taxes. These forms of businesses are handled differently in each state so professional help is advised.

An attorney can direct you about the types of incorporation available in your state, their advantages and disadvantages. A CPA can tell you how each type of incorporation is handled by the

IRS and your state if they impose an income tax. Sometimes you can get lucky and find a business attorney that is also a CPA.

### (iii) Trademark Your Company Name

Another possibility to consider is a trademark. You may be able to trademark your name and protect it federally and not just in your state. Contact the US Patent & Trademark Office in Washington, DC. Their 24 hour technical and general support number is 800-786-9199. Check www.uspto.gov to find information on why you should consider a trademark, how to file a trademark and the initial costs and fees.

# 6. Other Start-up Business Expenses

## (a) Insurance

A good liability policy is necessary to cover you and your business. If you are dealing with food, even though the manufacturer will be the ultimate target of any lawsuit, you can be sure that you will be named if something goes wrong. After all, the manufacturer doesn't know if you sold expired products to your customers or stored them improperly so their attorney will make sure that you are included in any action against the manufacturer.

Your inventory and products probably will not be covered under your normal homeowners policy. Likewise, customers picking up products at your home probably will not be covered. Tell your insurance agent what you want to do and be sure that it does not impact your current homeowners policy. Running a home-based business could possibly get your homeowner's policy canceled.

Ask about a product/company liability policy that will protect you and your personal assets in case of a lawsuit. Be sure to ask the agent when the policy is in force in case you change carriers. You can be covered under one policy, change companies and then have a problem come up later. Does the policy in force now cover your loss or will the old company be liable since you sold the basket before you changed insurance companies? Different policies are written different ways - just know the "what ifs" of a policy prior to taking it out or changing companies later.

Don't be afraid of asking questions like "If I sell the company and cancel the insurance and then a claim comes up, will the old insurance company handle it for me?" All insurance questions are valid so don't feel bad about asking them. If the agent does not know, get the main number to the insurance company and talk directly to an underwriter. The underwriter is not trying to sell you anything and knows more than the agent about the policy and the company. They will quickly tell you if a situation is covered. If you can't get the number from your agent, get another agent.

## (b) Separate Telephone Line

You will need a separate line from your home telephone. Currently, if you use your home telephone to conduct business you are not allowed a deduction for the cost of the telephone service.

Check with your local telephone company for prices on a second line but there are other options. Magic Jack (www.magicjack.com) can provide a great alternative if you have DSL service. The cost is about $50 for the equipment and first year's service and $20 a year after that. Buying multiple years worth of service will also save you money.

Ooma (www.ooma.com) is a similar service but costs a little more than the Magic Jack. Both will provide you with a separate telephone number without having to get a second line from your telephone service.

You can purchase a Tracfone (www.tracfone.com), a year's service and a 1000 minutes for about $100.

Since more people carry cell phones, the need for a 1-800 number is not as great as it once was. Check the costs with your telephone company. This may be something to add later but this should not be on your priority list.

Don't use your business line for personal calls no matter which system you choose.

Always answer in a happy, upbeat business like manner. Background noises should be nonexistent. Dogs barking, babies crying and background noise is not professional! If necessary, the telephone should be put in a room where you can shut the door before answering a business call.

## (c) Voice Mail

With the separate telephone service, you will also need voice mail. This service will assure you of getting missed telephone calls when you are busy with someone else. A regular answering machine will only pick up calls when you are not on the line.

Your message should include your hours of operation and your time zone. Leave an upbeat message letting them know you will call them back as soon as possible, or the next business day if it is after hours. Ask them to leave their time zone as well as their telephone number with their message, you don't want to wake them up the next morning! Your message should always be professional and should fit the season or upcoming holiday.

Make a special effort to check the voice mail if you have been on the telephone or out of the office. You can purchase a telephone with an indicator light when you have a message, but get into the habit of checking it anyway.

The Magic Jack, OOMA and Tracfone systems include voice mail and Magic Jack will send you an e-mail with the message attached.

## (d) Internet / DSL / Satellite Service

Regular dial up service may be acceptable at first, but the speed to upload your website and download your orders, will become an issue. DSL or Broadband would be better choices if available in your area. The slowest DSL service is usually many times faster than dial up, so try the slowest one first. Upgrade to a faster service if you need to later. Be sure to ask the telephone company if they offer a discounted package price with multiple services.

If you are out in the country where DSL or cable is not available, services like Hughes Net (www.hughesnet.com), Direct TV (www.directv.com) and Dish (www.dish.com) can provide satellite internet. This system requires professional installation and an exterior antenna. There is the possibility of disruption of service during heavy rainstorms. Since it is not tied to your telephone service, you will keep your connection even if the telephone service goes out. Expect to pay installation charges plus the cost of the equipment and around $60 per month in service, versus about $20 - 30 per month for DSL. Call and compare prices since this is a very competitive market with special pricing often being offered.

### (e) Shelving And Storage

Heavier weight metal shelving is best for items like cases of salsa. Plastic shelving, while easier to handle, will bow under the weight. Metal shelving usually can be adjusted to allow for larger boxes while plastic shelving spacing is usually set and can't be changed.

Before choosing your shelving, measure your boxes and then measure the shelves on the inside of the corner posts. A 36 inch shelf may only have a 32 inch usable opening. Also measure the usable space between the shelves.

I personally like a wide 24 inch deep shelf instead of the more common 18 inch deep shelf. I also like 5 shelves instead of 4 but these are taller.

### (f) Office Equipment

#### (i) Computer And Software

You will need one computer dedicated to your business. You do not want to have bits and pieces of your business, like e-mails and orders, on more than one machine.

A word processing and data base program should be sufficient software to start. You may want to add an accounting program later. If your computer did not come with the programs you need, check out Open Office (www.openoffice.org) or Libre (www.libreoffice.org). These are both free business suites with versions available for the Mac and Windows.

Most of your work will be on a hosted server, accessed through your internet browser. Your website, and the virtual terminal for receiving payments, will be accessed in this manner. Check with your hosting company and merchant account provider to be sure your particular browser will work with their systems. Download a new compatible browser if necessary.

If you are operating on a PC a virus service like McAfee is essential. If you are using a Mac the chances of getting a virus are less but protect your business and your customers. Intego (www.intego.com) has a virus program for the Mac and another for the Macs running windows. Your merchant account provider will usually require you to have, and keep updated, a virus program to protect their customers as part of the PCI protocol.

#### (ii) Printer, Copier And Fax Machine

An all-in-one machine is a great solution for a small office combining a scanner, copier & fax machine. An automatic document feed is a feature that will save time making copies or sending faxes with multiple pages. A machine with individual color cartridges has a cost advantage over one that has a single multiple color cartridge since only the color that runs out needs to be replaced. A quality color printer can be used for brochures and photo printing.

**Tip:** Save the empty ink jet cartridges in a zip lock bag and take them back to the office supply store. There are several large chain stores that will give you store credit for each one that you return. They have restrictions on how many you can return at once, and which brands they will accept, so ask. This may be something to remember when you purchase your new machine. If the store gives credit on a certain brand's used cartridges, and not on another, this may help you decide between brands. Make sure that all other features and actual costs are the same before letting this rebate/refund influence your decision.

Stores like Costco offer ink refills of old cartridges saving you money. This may void your warranty on a new machine so weigh your options and the cost savings.

Another option is a laser printer. Most laser printers only print in black and the machines and cartridges cost more, but overall per sheet printing costs are much less than ink jet printers. Color laser printers are available but are very expensive. You may want to invest in a laser printer for the bulk of your office needs and a color ink jet reserved for photos and brochures.

### (g) PO Box Rental

It is mandatory that contact information be posted on your website. A PO box is essential if you are e-commerce only. You want your customers to know exactly where you are if you have a brick and mortar storefront, but if you are e-commerce only, <u>do not</u> put your home address on the internet! A small PO Box costs about $65 per year.

# 7. Money Matters

Open a company bank account and get a business credit card as soon as you can to establish the separation between your personal expenses and the company's. You must keep detailed records of all company expenses and receipts.

<u>Don't use the company's accounts to pay your personal bills.</u> If you need a draw, make the check out to yourself and then cash the check or deposit it into your personal account.

### (a) Business Bank Account

A dedicated bank account will keep all of the business expenses separate. To open the account in your company's name, you will need to provide the bank with your DBA certificate or incorporation papers. The account should use your IRS issued ID number or company's EIN number instead of your social security number. Laws vary so provide any documentation that the bank may need.

There is a great deal of competition between the banks so you should be able to find a business account with no monthly fees and with no minimum balance. Some banks are offering the first set of checks free. If your bank insists on charging you by the item, either deposited or debited, a monthly fee and other major fees because it is considered a commercial account, check around. There are banks that would love to have your business and they are making deals to get it!

Open your business checking account prior to applying for your merchant account since it will be used to deposit your daily sales directly.

### (b) Company Credit Card

While I am partial to American Express (www.americanexpress.com), some companies will not accept it as readily as a Visa or MasterCard. Contact American Express at 1-800-519-OPEN (6736) to apply for a small business credit card.

The American Express Blue For Business earns points for every dollar you spend and the Plum Card gives you cash back for paying your balance early. These cards allow you to carry a balance to the next month if you must and have no annual fee. The interest on the card is very high, encouraging you to pay the balance in full each month.

Visa and MasterCard both have business cards with rewards. Contact your local bank to apply for a company Visa or MasterCard and compare several cards for the best rates and features.

### (c) Getting Paid

### (i) Accounts Receivable

I am going to suggest that you never take a Purchase Order or other payment arrangement from your customers. I can hear other business owners screaming at this statement, but you should not have to worry about collecting your money.

While I was in business, dealing with some of the biggest companies in the USA, we were always paid in advance. Most of the executives that I worked with purchased gifts on their personal credit card and then they would submit an expense report to their company to be reimbursed.

I can not stress enough - get your money prior to sending out your baskets. Don't waste your time worrying about when, or if, you will get your money prior to your bills coming due.

You are not alone in this policy. When you call the florist or place an order online, you are always asked for your payment prior to completing the order. Do not let a company convince you to take a purchase order or get you to bill them for all of their gifts once a month. You don't need the extra paperwork or the headache of getting your payment. If they will not do business with your company because of this policy, let them go elsewhere and concentrate on the companies that do not mind paying for what they get, when they get it.

Decide for yourself whether to carry customer accounts or insist on payment up front, but I never had a problem or a complaint when I asked "and which credit card would you like to use today?" I did not carry any accounts receivable on my books and I suggest you don't.

### (ii) Your Merchant Account

You need to be able to accept credit cards from your customers. It is even more important if your business solely operates on the internet.

MasterCard & Visa are the most popular with individuals. However, if the majority of your customers are corporations, American Express is a necessity. There are others like Discover Card you might consider if they have no additional fees other than the discount rate. Each of these cards have their own rules and fees and your merchant account provider can help you decide.

You can become established as a merchant with American Express (www.americanexpress.com) by calling them directly at 855-894-6570. They have two pricing plans at this time - one is the Flat Fee Plan at $7.95 per month with no additional charges. Amex also has a standard merchant account that charges a percentage of your Amex sales with no additional fees or charges.

In years of doing business with American Express, I experienced only one rate change and it was a decrease in my rate! They have the same rate for all cards accepted, no monthly minimums, no monthly fees or annual fees.

Once set up with American Express list your company in their merchant directory and receive some free advertising. Merchant services telephone number is 800-528-5200.

The best way to locate a merchant account provider for MasterCard and Visa is to call the banks in your area and ask them who they recommend. Get quotes on start up fees, their monthly minimum, monthly statement fees, how much they charge per transaction and any additional fees for accepting rewards cards. It is very important to ask about termination or cancelation fees if you want to change providers or if you go out of business. Most want hundreds of dollars to let you out of your contract, even if you go out of business.

Be sure they provide everything to you in writing and that there are no other pages to the contract. I have heard of companies getting you to sign the 2 pages of the contract that lists the majority of the fees, but they don't send you the actual 12 page contract until you have signed what you thought was the complete contract. Get them to send you everything prior to signing anything. If they will not provide this to you, look for another provider quick!

If you belong to Costco or Sam's Club, they have merchant account providers for their business members.

Your merchant account provider may want to set you up using a credit card machine. Usually these cost between $300-600 or can be leased on a monthly basis but require a dedicated telephone line. If most of your sales are going to be through the internet or by telephone, I personally think a credit card machine is unnecessary.

A better option, and one that I personally used and loved, is called a Virtual Terminal (VT). You log into a secure site, input the customers information and process the transaction on the internet. The company will provide you with training prior to your first transaction. They also provide 24 hour telephone support for their VT customers. You can print out your receipt, a customer's receipt, run different reports and do transaction searches if needed. This is a great tool and I highly recommend it. The cost for the virtual terminal is usually free to the merchant, but check with your particular processor.

25

If you are an internet only business you will be classified as 'mail order telephone order' (MOTO) or also referred to as 'card not present' and your transaction fees are going to cost more.

The fees that you are quoted for processing cards will be expressed in percentage of the total order. Your rate will be established in the contract with your processor and usually depend on how much business you expect to do and how long you have been in business. Keep in mind that even though you have a contracted amount, this amount will change if Visa or MasterCard raise their rates, but you should be given written notice of any increase. Most of the time these notices are on your monthly statement, so be sure to read every page.

One thing that you will find on your statement that will probably raise your blood pressure a notch or two is the additional fees that your contract mentions, but does not tell you how much - because they don't know. I have gotten statements that correctly charged us 2.25% for a certain transaction and then on the second page we were charged an additional 1.4% because the card was a certain type of business card or a rewards card. You can not ask what type of card is being used for a transaction and you can not refuse to take a certain card. It is a shock when you are charged almost 4% for a transaction when you are expecting your contracted 2.25%!

When you call the processor they will quickly tell you that they are "just passing along the fees that Visa and MasterCard charge them for certain special cards." Nothing they can do about this and nothing you can do about it either. I know that you have a contracted amount, but use this figure as a starting point of your fees. This is where American Express shines. Yes, their discount rate is higher, but they do not add these hidden fees - if they quote 3% it is 3% - period.

Check with American Express and your merchant account provider as to when you will be paid. Usually Visa and MasterCard pay their merchants in two days and American Express in three. Also ask if their fees will be taken out on a daily basis, before your deposit, or will they be taken out in a single withdrawal at the end of the month? Call your bank each morning and get that day's deposits. Verify the deposit with what you processed a couple of days ago. Your VT will be very helpful in verifying that you have been paid for each transaction.

When you set up your merchant account, ask what information you must keep and for how long. Once this period is past, the information should be shredded for security reasons. You don't want personal credit card information accessible to anyone in the office or to thieves, but the credit card companies may require certain information be kept for audit purposes. Be sure to comply with any and all credit card requirements.

There are other ways to process cards without actually having a merchant account. PayPal (www.paypal.com), Amazon Payments (https://payments.amazon.com) and Google Checkout (www.checkout.google.com), are three other systems for you to investigate. These systems allow you to get paid by clients using their credit cards but you never see their information, it is taken care of behind the scenes. This is safer for your customers and for you. Since you do not have access to the actual credit card information, you can't lose it or have someone steal the information from you.

Once your merchant account is set up, you may be tempted to set up your shopping cart to automatically processes the credit cards using a gateway. This gateway is another function, and usually costs about $25 additional per month. I do not recommend a gateway or charging the credit cards immediately. Here are a few reasons why:

Let's say that you are having a very good month and your supplies are running low. All of a sudden the telephone is ringing off the wall, your computer is full of orders, a national magazine has just reviewed your products and now everyone wants one! You are flooded with orders, you have no supplies and no help. A situation that in some respects would be heaven sent, however, not today!

If your shopping cart is accepting orders and charging the cards automatically, what do you do when there is no way to deliver? First you have to suspend your website so no new orders can be taken, contact all of the customers and cancel the orders and then credit every one of those cards. Did you know that you pay the processing fee to the credit card company for taking the card and then you have to pay it again to credit that card? So now you have lost orders, had to pay double credit card processing fees with no income, and had to take all that time just to handle the credits and the chaos.....no thanks!

A better system would be to set up your shopping cart for 'simple validation' or 'offline credit card processing' function. This allows you to process the credit cards when the baskets are shipped. If you are overrun by orders, contact your customers by e-mail letting them know of a slight delay and assure them their card has not been charged and you will get their basket out as soon as possible. This will give you a couple of days to get supplies in and the baskets out. If this is not acceptable, the customer can cancel the order and no refund is due since their card was not automatically charged.

Since some of your customers will want changes to their baskets - take out the chili and add another coffee and package of pecans - the fact that you do not automatically charge the cards allows you the flexibility to correct the amount for a customized basket. If the customer wants the basket sent Next Day Air you can easily quote the fee and adjust the basket price and charge the correct amount to their credit card the first time.

This method also has an advantage at Christmas. Most customers will eagerly order early knowing their credit card will not be charged until their order goes out in a few weeks. This pre-ordering helps you plan your inventory purchases more accurately for the Christmas rush.

### (d) Checks

Most people will provide you with a credit card number but some will want to pay with a check. I made it a policy not to take checks unless it was a corporate client that requested to pay by check.

Individual checks from local people will be something you will need to decide for yourself. Where a credit card gives you immediate payment approval, a check will take several days to clear the bank and by that time you have sent out the basket and paid the shipping company. If you don't want the worry of collecting your money later, think about a cash or credit card only policy.

### (e) Inventory Replacement

Replace your regular inventory after you have paid your expenses for the month. By purchasing items in case lots, it doesn't take long to eat up profits. While your new company is getting established, replace your inventory stock and allow a certain amount each month to go to increasing and growing your inventory. Perhaps add a new product each month and highlight it on your website. The more choices you give your customers, the happier they will be.

After you have gone through a season or two and gotten an idea of what sells, start buying out of season merchandise for next year. Items like gift cards and holiday cellophane wrap can be a bargain at the end of the season.

Nashville Wraps has wonderful sales between seasons and right after the holidays. Sign up to be notified since the specials only last until the merchandise is gone.

I have purchased some wonderful wrap, gift cards and tags this way at a fraction of the cost. You have to be willing to invest in inventory that you may not use for a year. If you have a storage issue, be selective in the items that you purchase out of season. Keep cellophane in its original sealed container since it attracts dust like a magnet. Buying out of season can really help in next year's profit margin.

<u>Inventory Tip:</u> If you live in a state or county that assess taxes on what you have in inventory on January 1st, wait until January 2nd to replace your depleted inventory stock from the Christmas season.

## (f) Accounting Matters

Accounting is such an important part of any successful business. It is a touchy subject for many business people because they say they are too busy earning a living to keep up with the books. Try not to be one of these people. If you don't know if you are making money or losing it, how can you adjust your actions to fix any problems?

Be diligent about keeping the records current on a daily basis no matter which method you use. Try to put everything down as it happens - deposits made, checks written and product orders taken. A few minutes reserved for this task at the close of the day is a great habit to get into.

If you are comfortable using the computer, an accounting program may be a good solution. Find one that can be adjusted to your business needs and particular expenses. Check out WaveApps (www.waveapps.com), a website that provides free software for accounting, invoicing and payroll functions for business and personal needs.

For a beginners guide to bookkeeping check out www.fastpathbooks.com. Great information if you need this information or would like an accounting refresher. This website uses the Express Accounting Software (www.nchsoftware.com) during its demonstrations but the actual information presented pertains to accounting standards and not just to an individual system or program. Covers the basics, types of accounts you will need and transaction reporting, taxes, depreciation, journals entries and different needed reports.

If you are uncomfortable with doing it yourself let a CPA set up your books in the beginning and, if necessary, handle the bookkeeping for you during the year. This is an area that a professional can truly save you money and point out any trouble spots along the way. WaveApps (www.waveapps.com) has a link called "find a pro" which will locate a professional in your area. Ask other business people for referrals for a CPA or bookkeeper in your area. You need to feel comfortable with that individual because you will be sharing your financial records and business details with them.

I prefer to handle the bookkeeping by hand. Most office supply stores carry the Dome brand of bookkeeping records and it is a great tool. Basically a fill in the blank book that you can adjust to your needs. There is one for monthly accounting and one for weekly. Cost is about $15 per book.

The following examples can be used to make your own individual sheets on the computer and then fill them in by hand. There should be a sheet for operating expenses and other notations, a sheet for your inventory purchases, an income ledger and a summary sheet for each month of the year. Make as many lines as necessary. Adjust the sheets for your business needs and after talking to your CPA.

Items you will need to keep track of on a monthly basis:

Expense Ledger                                Date:_____

Date Paid / Company Paid / Item Purchased / Check/Cash/CC / Account # / Amount

1)

2)

3)


Business Equipment and Assets Ledger          Date:_____

Date Paid / Company Paid / Item Purchased / Check/Cash/CC / Amount

1)

2)

3)


Inventory Purchases                           Date:_____

Date Paid / Company Paid / Item Purchased / Check/Cash/CC / Amount

1)

2)

3)


Sales Receipts for the month of: _____

Customer Name / Invoice Number / Which credit card / Amount

1)

2)

3)

Business Expense Summary for the month of: _____

Accounting Fees:

Advertising Expenses:

Cash Contributions:

Commissions Paid:

Contract Labor:

Delivery Expense - In:

Delivery Expenses - Out:

DSL / Internet Access:

Insurance:

Interest:

Legal Expenses:

Licenses:

Membership/Trade Dues:

Merchant Account Fees:

Misc.

Office Expenses:

Postage:

Rental fees:

     Office space:

     Equipment:

Repairs:

Taxes Paid:

     Sales Taxes:

     Employee Taxes:

     Other:

Supplies:

Telephone:

Utilities:

Web Hosting Expenses:


Summary:

Gross receipts and sales for the month:_____


Business Expenses for the month:_____


Inventory Purchased for the month:_____


Business equipment and other assets for the month:_____


Other notations:

    Business miles driven this month:_____


    Cash on Hand:_____


    Owner's Equity/ Capital Account:_____


    Equipment / Depreciation:_____


    Liabilities / Loans:_____

# Chapter 3
## Locating Your Products

Finding suppliers close to your location is to your advantage. Sometimes this is not possible but always try to find outlets within driving distance. This is especially true with heavy items. Products such as a case of 12 - 16 oz salsas will cost you dearly to ship and will diminish your profit margin. Local suppliers will be a blessing in the busy times and for large, unexpected custom orders.

With a local supplier, you can usually call ahead and pick up your products if a large rush order comes in or if you are low on products. They know you by name and will do all they can to help you succeed.

Since you will be dealing with smaller manufacturers, you might be dealing directly with the owner of the company. If you are dealing with the owner or manager, and they take credit cards, ask for a cash discount if you pay with a check or cash. They may extend a credit equal to the percentage that they would have paid to accept your credit card, usually around 4 - 5%. Any other employee may not have the authority to grant such a discount. Sometimes smaller companies run on very tight budgets, so getting their money immediately may be worth the discount to them, so ask.

## 1. State Agricultural Departments And Programs

Since you are establishing a regional gift basket business, the best place to find your gourmet food products is to start with your state's Department of Agriculture. This agency helps farmers and ranchers market their products and most have a logo or branding program you can join. These programs are usually developed and managed by the marketing division. You can call the agency for assistance or search their member list online for products.

Consider joining your state's program. Your membership may be a full membership or an associate membership since you are not actually producing the products that you will sell. Some of the states have a specific "Gift Basket" category on their site. After all, you are supporting and promoting the products made in your state too! Oklahoma is one of these and they have a great site!

These programs often provide product stickers with the program's logo, brochures and other advertising materials to their members. Some programs offer excellent marketing opportunities in regional magazines and print, at trade shows, food events and state fairs at discounted rates and located under the Agricultural Department's banner. In some cases these programs provide matching advertising funds.

In Texas we have the "Go Texan" program. A company can join and promote their products in the state, the US and internationally. To be a member you have to produce your products in the state or process them here. Many of the companies are family run farms that grow, package and sell their items right at their location - anything from flavored pecans to stone ground cornmeal. You can also be a member if your product consists mainly of other member's products, such as a gift basket.

I used the "Go Texan" website as the main resource for my business. With a click of my mouse I had access to regional products I didn't know existed. Links to the companies are on their individual pages and with a quick e-mail or telephone call, samples and information arrived from all over the state in days.

The companies that you will be working with will be the actual growers and manufacturers of the products. Some will be happy to work with you and others will refer you to their sales reps. If they have a website, ask to be listed as a location to buy their products. Most will be happy to do this and some will provide a link to your website.

* * * * * *

The following is a list of states' Department of Agriculture with contact information and website addresses. Some of the states are still developing their programs and others only provide limited support, but they are constantly being improved and changed. Contact them about what is currently available and how the marketing department can assist you in promoting your business or finding great products.

Information for other sources that you may find helpful is listed here as well. These sources could be Specialty Food Associations or community kitchens set up to help small companies produce their products.

* * * * * *

Directories & State Resources

Agricultural Marketing Resource Center
http://www.agmrc.org/directories_state_resources/

Food Industry Market Maker
www.national.marketmaker.uiuc.edu


Alabama
http://www.agi.state.al.us/
Alabama Department of Agriculture & Industries
1445 Federal Drive, Montgomery, AL 36107
Telephone: 334-240-7171 / 205-823-5498 / 1-800-642-7761
Agriculture Promotion Division
Telephone: 334-240-7249
Buy Alabama's Best
www.buyalabamasbest.com
Telephone: 205-823-8544
E-mail: info@buyalabamasbest.com
This is a partnership of the Dept. of Ag, the Alabama Grocers Assoc. and the Alabama Food
Manufacturers and Producers.

Alaska
www.dnr.alaska.gov
Alaska Division of Agriculture
Main Office:
1800 Glenn Highway, Suite 12, Palmer, Alaska 99645
Telephone: 907-745-7200
Alaska Grown
www.alaskagrown.org

Arizona
www.azda.gov
Arizona Department of Agriculture
1688 West Adams Street, Phoenix, AZ 85007
Telephone: 602-542-0904
At the time of this writing there is an Arizona Grown program logo that you can use with no fee or
membership, but the program is not being actively marketed by the Agricultural Department. Go to
the site or call for any updates to their programs.

Also check out:


Flavors of Arizona
www.flavorsofarizona.org
PO Box 28247, Scottsdale, AZ 85255
Telephone: 480-473-0285
Organization of Arizona food manufacturers which promotes the sale and consumption of Arizona processed food products.


Arkansas
www.aad.arkansas.gov
Arkansas Agricultural Department
#1 Natural Resources Drive, Little Rock, AR 72205
Telephone: 501-219-6324
Arkansas Grown
www.arkansasgrown.org

California
http://www.cdfa.ca.gov
Buy California Marketing Agreement
1521 I St, Sacramento CA 95814
Telephone: 916-654-0466
California Grown
www.californiagrown.org
E-mail: info@californiagrown.org

Colorado
www.colorado.gov/ag
Colorado Department of Agriculture
700 Kipling St., Suite 4000, Lakewood, CO 80215
Telephone: 303-239-4100
Markets Division
Telephone: 303-239-4119
Colorado Proud
www.coloradoproud.org

Also check out:

Colorado MarketMaker
www.comarketmaker.com

Connecticut
www.ct.gov/doag
Department of Agriculture
165 Capitol Avenue, Hartford, CT 06106
Telephone:  860-713-2500
Connecticut Grown
www.ctgrown.gov
Telephone:  860-713-2558

Also check out:

Connecticut Food Association
www.ctfood.org
195 Farmington Avenue, Suite 200, Farmington, CT  06032
Telephone:  860-677-8097
Searchable membership directory.
Connecticut Specialty Food Association
www.connecticutspecialtyfood.com

Also check out:

Harvest NE Assoc., Inc.
www.harvestnewengland.org
Agricultural Departments of Connecticut, Maine, Massachusetts, New Hampshire, Rhode Island and
Vermont.

Delaware
www.dda.delaware.gov
Delaware Department of Agriculture
2320 South DuPont Highway, Dover, Delaware 19901
Telephone:  302-698-4500 / 800-282-8685 (In Dclaware only)
Delaware Made
www.delawaremade.com

Florida
www.florida-agriculture.com
Florida Department of Agriculture and Consumer Services
Division of Marketing and Development
Mayo Building
407 South Calhoun Street, Fourth Floor, M9, Tallahassee, Florida  32399-0800
Fresh from Florida
www.florida-agriulture.com/marketing/fapc.htm

For Producers and Specialty - for business - Florida Ag. promotional campaign. FAPC Member Search. The division administers the Florida Agricultural Promotional Campaign (FAPC), also known as "Fresh from Florida" that assists the state's agricultural producers in expanding markets.

Georgia
www.agr.georgia.gov
Georgia Department of Agriculture
19 Martin Luther King, Jr. Dr., S.W., Room 232, Atlanta, Georgia  30334
Telephone: 404-656-3680
Marketing Division
Telephone:  404-656-3740
Georgia Grown
www.georgiagrown.com
New website and search feature.

Hawaii
www.hawaii.gov/hdoa
Hawaii Department of Agriculture
1428 S. King Street, Honolulu, HI 96814-2512
Telephone:  808-973-9560
E-mail:  hdoa.info@hawaii.gov
Agricultural Development Division
Market Development Branch
Telephone:  808-973-9627
E-mail:  hdoa.md@hawaii.gov
Seal of Quality Program
Call for more details.

Also check out:

Hawaii Food Manufacturers Association
www.foodsofhawaii.com

Idaho
www.agri.state.id.us
Idaho State Department of Agriculture
2270 Old Penitentiary Road, Boise, Idaho 83712
Telephone:  208-332-8542
E-mail:  info@agri.idaho.gov
Idaho Preferred
www.idahopreferred.com

Illinois
www.agr.state.il.us
State of Illinois Department of Agriculture
State Fairgrounds
P.O. Box 19281, Springfield, IL  62794-9281
Telephone: 217-782-2172
Bureau of Marketing and Promotion
Telephone:  217-524-3297
E-mail:  agr.ilproductslogo@illinois.gov
Illinois Product Logo Program
www.agr.state.il.us/marketing/ilprodlogo/index.html
To search for products:    www.agr.state.il.us/markets/mis/index.php
Use of the logo is free of charge. Go to the website, click on marketing and you will see a screen with the Illinois product logo.  Click on the logo and it will take you to the program.  The Illinois Food and Agribusiness Guide lists about 1500 companies.


Indiana
www.in.gov/isda/
Indiana State Department of Agriculture
1 North Capitol, Suite 600, Indianapolis, IN  46204
Telephone:  317-232-8770
E-mail:  communications@isda.in.gov


Iowa
www.iowa.gov/agriculture_and_natural_resources
www.iowaagriculture.gov
IDALS
Iowa Department of Agriculture and Land Stewardship
Wallace State Office Building,
502 E. 9th Street,  Des Moines, IA 50319
Telephone:  515-281-5321
E-mail:  agmarketing@iowaagriculture.gov


Kansas
www.ksda.gov
Kansas Department of Agriculture
109 S.W. 9th Street, 4th Floor, Topeka, KS  66612
E-mail:  ksag@kda.ks.gov
Kansas Department of Commerce - Agriculture Marketing Division
Telephone:  785-296-6080
Simply Kansas
www.simplykansas.com

Kentucky
http://www.kyagr.com/
Kentucky Department of Agriculture
Office Of The Commissioner
111 Corporate Drive, Frankfort, KY  40601
Telephone:  502-564-4696
Office of Ag Marketing
100 Fair Oaks, 5th Floor, Frankfort, KY  40601
Telephone:  502-564-4983
Kentucky Proud
www.kyproud.com
Member index and product search.

Louisiana
www.ldaf.state.la.us
Louisiana Dept. of Agriculture & Forestry
5825 Florida Boulevard, Baton Rouge, Louisiana 70806
Telephone:  866-927-2476 / 225-922-1234
E-mail:  info@ldaf.state.la.us
Marketing and Agricultural Economic Development
Telephone: 225-922-1234 / 225-922-1280
Certified Product of Louisiana
Certified Cajun Product of Louisiana
Certified Creole Product of Louisiana
www.ldaf.state.la.us/portal/offices/marketingagriculturaleconomicdevelopment/certifiedlogos/tabid/
322/default.aspx
There is a link to their Louisiana Products Directory, both food and non food, on the website which
can be downloaded in PDF format:
http://www.ldaf.state.la.us/portal/offices/marketingagriculturaleconomicdevelopment/
marketdevelopment/louisianatradedirectory/tabid/335/default.aspx

Maine
www.maine.gov/agriculture/index.shtml
Maine Department of Agriculture
28 State House Station, Deering Bldg. - AMHI Complex
90 Blossom Lane, Augusta, ME  04333-0028
Telephone:  207-287-3200
Division of Market and Production Development
Telephone:  207-287-3491
Get Real Maine
www.getrealmaine.com

Also check out:

Harvest NE Assoc., Inc.
www.harvestnewengland.org
Agricultural Departments of Connecticut, Maine, Massachusetts, New Hampshire, Rhode Island and Vermont.

Maryland
www.mda.state.md.us/
Maryland Department of Agriculture
50 Harry S. Truman Parkway, Annapolis, MD 21401
Telephone: 410-841-5770
Marketing and Agribusiness Development
Telephone: 410-841-5770
Maryland's Best
www.marylandsbest.net
E-mail: marylandsbest@maryland.gov
Mainly fresh produce but does include processed items. There is a wholesale search on the site and a Buyer - Grower Directory in PDF format.

Massachusetts
www.mass.gov/agr
Massachusetts Department of Agricultural Resources
251 Causeway Street, Suite 500, Boston, MA 02114
Telephone: 617-626-1753

Massachusetts Grown & Fresher
www.massgrown.org

Also check out:

Harvest NE Assoc., Inc.
www.harvestnewengland.org
Agricultural Departments of Connecticut, Maine, Massachusetts, New Hampshire, Rhode Island and Vermont.

The Massachusetts Specialty Food Association
www.msfa.net
PO Box 34, Groton, MA 01450
Telephone: 508-457-5346 / 800-813-5862
Member directory. Associate members list companies furnishing labels, packaging, etc.

Michigan
www.michigan.gov/mda
Michigan Department of Agriculture and Rural Development
P.O. Box 30017, Lansing, Michigan 48909
Telephone: 517-373-9789 / 800-292-3939
E-mail: mda-info@michigan.gov
As of this writing, there does not appear to be a logo program, but check for updates with their marketing department.

Also check out:

Buy Michigan Now
PO Box 511135
Livonia, MI 48151
www.buymichigannow.com
Searchable directory of products and members. They have different levels of membership for you to join with your gift basket business.

Making It In Michigan
www.Makingitinmichigan.msu.edu
Premier specialty food show

Minnesota
www.mda.state.mn.us
Minnesota Department of Agriculture
625 N. Robert Street, St. Paul, Minnesota 55155
Telephone: 651-201-6170 / 800-967-2474
Marketing Services Division
Minnesota Grown
www.minnesotagrown.com
There is a product search on the website or you can order the printed Minnesota Grown Directory:
www.mda.state.mn.us/food/minnesotagrown/mgdorderform.aspx
Copies are also available at local Chamber of Commerce Travel Info Centers or at your library.

Mississippi
www.mdac.state.ms.us
Mississippi Department of Agriculture & Commerce
121 N. Jefferson Street, Jackson, MS 39201
Telephone: 601-359-1100
Market Development
Telephone: 601-359-1163
Make Mine Mississippi
www.mdac.state.ms.us/departments/marketing/make-mine-mississippi.htm

Missouri
www.mda.mo.gov
Missouri Department of Agriculture
1616 Missouri Boulevard
Jefferson City, Missouri 65102
Telephone: 573-751-4211
Agrimissouri
www.agrimissouri.com
Product search: www.agrimissouri.com/mo-made
Telephone: 573-522-3169 / 573-522-9213

Montana
www.agr.mt.gov
Montana Department of Agriculture
302 N. Roberts Street, Helena, Montana 59601
Telephone: 406-444-3144
E-mail: agr@mt.gov
Agriculture Development Division
Telephone: 406-444-2402

Nebraska
www.agr.state.ne.us
Nebraska Department of Agriculture
301 Centennial Mall South, Lincoln, NE 68509-4947
Telephone: 402-471-2341
E-mail: agr.webmaster@nebraska.gov
Ag Promotion and Development
Telephone: 402-471-4876 / 800-422-6692
There is a holiday list in PDF format: www.agr.ne.gov/publications/promotion/holiday.pdf

Also, check out:

Grow Nebraska
www.grownebraska.org
The Grow Nebraska is a non-profit program in partnership with the Nebraska Department of
Economic Development.

Nevada
www.agri.state.nv.us
Nevada Department of Agriculture
405 South 21st. Street, Sparks, NV 89431
Telephone: 775-353-3600

Nevada Grown
www.nevadagrown.com
The Nevada Grown program was developed by the Business Services Group with funding from the Nevada Department of Agriculture.
PO Box 2108, Sparks, NV 89432
Telephone: 775-351-2551

Also check out:

Made in Nevada
www.madeinnevada.org
P.O. Box 1268, Carson City, NV 89702
Telephone: 775-315-5718
E-mail: info@madeinnevada.org
Made in Nevada is a marketing initiative funded by cooperating businesses and sponsors and wholly-owned, governed, and managed by participating business. Advertising, promotional events, education and market development of Nevada-made products.


New Hampshire
www.agriculture.nh.gov
New Hampshire Department of Agriculture, Markets & Food
25 Capitol Street, 2nd Floor, Concord, NH 03302
Telephone: 603-271-3551
Division of Agricultural Development
Telephone: 603-271-3788

Also check out:

Harvest NE Assoc., Inc.
www.harvestnewengland.org
Agricultural Dept. of Connecticut, Maine, Massachusetts, New Hampshire, Rhode Island and Vermont.


New Hampshire Made
www.nhmade.com
539 Calef Hwy, Rte 125 #104, Epping, NH 03042
Telephone: 603-679-9800
E-mail: info@nhmade.com
New Hampshire Made is a privately funded co-operative, a public / private partnership.

New Jersey
www.state.nj.us/agriculture
State of New Jersey Department of Agriculture
PO Box 330, Trenton, NJ 08625
Telephone: 609-292-3976
Division of Marketing & Development
Telephone: 609-292-5536
Jersey Fresh
www.jerseyfresh.nj.gov
A new website is planned describing their "Made with Jersey Fresh" program and listing value-added processed products.


Also, check out:


The NJ Food Processors Association
www.njfoodprocessors.org

The Rutgers Food Innovation Center
www.foodinnovation.rutgers.edu/index.html
Telephone: 856-459-1900

New Mexico
www.nmdaweb.nmsu.edu
New Mexico Department of Agriculture
MSC 3189, Box 30005, Las Cruces, NM 88003-8005
Telephone: 575-646-3007
Marketing and Development Division
MSC 5600, PO Box 30005, Las Cruces, NM 88003-8005
Telephone: 575-646-4929
Taste the Tradition and Grown with Tradition
www.newmexicotradition.com


Also check out:


New Mexico Specialty Foods
www.newmexicospecialtyfoods.com
E-mail: info@newmexicospecialtyfoods.com
85 Companies that produce New Mexico products.

New York
www.agriculture.ny.gov
New York State Department of Agriculture & Markets
10B Airline Drive Albany, NY 12235
Telephone: 800-554-4501
E-mail: info@agriculture.ny.gov
Pride of New York
www.prideofny.com
10B Airline Drive, Albany, NY 12235
Telephone: 800-554-4501
E-mail: prideofny@agriculture.ny.gov

North Carolina
www.ncagr.gov
North Carolina Department of Agriculture & Consumer Services
2 West Edenton Street, Raleigh, NC 27601
Telephone: 919-707-3000
Marketing Division
Telephone: 919-707-3100
Goodness Grows in North Carolina   and   Got To Be North Carolina
www.gottobenc.com
Telephone: 919-233-7887 ext. 278

Also check out:

North Carolina Specialty Foods Association
www.ncspecialtyfoods.org
PO Box 6549, Raleigh, NC 27628
Telephone: 919-961-0880 / 919-880-9889
Numerous benefits as a retail member - $20 membership fee - many manufacturers to select your products from.

North Dakota
www.nd.gov/ndda
North Dakota Department of Agriculture
600 E. Boulevard Ave, Department 602, Bismarck, ND 58505-0020
Telephone: 701-328-2231 / 800-242-7535
E-mail: ndda@nd.gov
Marketing Division
Pride of Dakota
www.prideofdakota.com
E-mail: prideofdakota@gmail.com

Ohio
www.ohioagriculture.gov/
Ohio Department of Agriculture
8995 E. Main Street, Reynoldsburg, OH 43068-3399
Telephone: 614-728-6201
agri@agri.ohio.gov
Marketing Division
E-mail: markets@agri.ohio.gov
Ohio Proud
www.ohioproud.org
E-mail: ohioproud@agri.ohio.gov
Telephone: 800-467-7683
Gift Basket Companies can be affiliate members.

Oklahoma
www.state.ok.us/~okag
Oklahoma Department of Agriculture, Food, and Forestry
2800 N. Lincoln Blvd, Oklahoma City, OK 73105
Telephone: 405-521-3864
Market Development Services Division
www.state.ok.us/~okag/mktdev
Telephone: 405-522-5560
Made In Oklahoma
www.madeinoklahoma.net
Actual gift basket directory on the site - great searchable site!

Oregon
www.oregon.gov/oda
Oregon Department of Agriculture
635 Capitol St. NE, Salem, Oregon USA 97301-2532
info@oda.state.or.us
Telephone: 503-986-4550
Agricultural Development and Marketing
E-mail: agmarket@oda.state.or.us
Telephone: 503-872-6600

Also check out:

Northwest Specialty Foods Association and Agri-Business Council of Oregon
www.nwspecialtyfoods.org
1200 NW Naito Parkway #290, Portland, OR 97209
Telephone: 503-241-1487
Association between Oregon and Washington businesses.

Pennsylvania
www.agric.state.pa.us
Pennsylvania Department of Agriculture
2301 North Cameron Street, Harrisburg, PA 17110
Telephone: 717-787-4737
Bureau of Market Development
Telephone: 717-787-5643 / 888-724-7697
E-mail: ra-markets@pa.gov
Pennsylvania Preferred
Telephone: 717-705-3928
www.agric.state.pa.us/papreferred.com
Searchable site: http://www.agric.state.pa.us/papreferred/search.aspx

Rhode Island
www.dem.ri.gov/programs/bnatres/agricult/index.htm
Department of Environmental Management - Division of Agriculture
235 Promenade Street, Providence, RI 02908-5767
Telephone: 401-222-2781
Marketing & Promotion
Telephone: 401-222-2781 ext. 4517
Farm Fresh Rhode Island
www.farmfreshri.org
1005 Main St., #1220, Pawtucket, RI 02860
Telephone: 401-312-4250

Also check out:

Harvest NE Assoc., Inc.
www.harvestnewengland.org
Agricultural Departments of Connecticut, Maine, Massachusetts, New Hampshire, Rhode Island and
Vermont.

RI Local Food Guide
www.farmfresh.org

South Carolina
www.agriculture.sc.gov
South Carolina Department of Agriculture
PO Box 11280, Columbia, SC 29211
Telephone: 803-734-2210
Certified South Carolina
www.certifiedscgrown.com

Also check out:

South Carolina Specialty Food Association
www.scsfa.org
Great product resource.


South Dakota
www.sdda.sd.gov
South Dakota Department of Agriculture
523 E Capitol Ave, Pierre, SD 57501-3182
Telephone:  605-773-3375  /  800-228-5254 (in state)
E-mail:  agmail@state.sd.us
Value Added Ag Development
Telephone:  605-773-5146  /  800-228-5254
E-mail:  dakotaflavor@state.sd.us
South Dakota Flavor!
www.dakotaflavor.com
Made In South Dakota
www.madeinsouthdakota.com
Telephone:  800-872-6190


Tennessee
www.state.tn.us/agriculture
Tennessee Department of Agriculture
Ellington Agricultural Center
440 Hogan Road, Nashville, TN 37220-9029
Telephone:  615-837-5103
Market Development Division
Telephone:  615-837-5160
Processed & Gourmet Foods Marketing Specialist
Telephone:  615-837-5345
Pick Tennessee Products
www.picktnproducts.org

Also check out:


Tennessee Specialty Food Association Inc. (TSFA)
www.tsfagourment.com
Telephone:  931-294-5906

Texas
www.texasagriculture.gov
1700 N. Congress, 11th Floor, Austin, TX 78701
Telephone: 512-463-7476 / Nationwide Toll Free: 800-TELL-TDA (835-5832)
E-mail: customer.relations@texasagriculture.gov
Marketing & International Trade
Telephone: 877-99-GOTEX
GO TEXAN
www.gotexan.org
E-mail: gotexan@texasagriculture.gov
Excellent product and company search with hundreds of companies.

Utah
www.ag.utah.gov
Utah Department of Agriculture and Food
350 North Redwood Road, Salt Lake City, UT 84116
Telephone: 801-538-7100
E-mail: agriculture@utah.gov
Marketing and Development Division
Telephone: 801-538-7108
Utah's Own
www.utahsown.utah.gov
Telephone: 801-538-7141


Vermont
www.vermontagriculture.com
Vermont Agency of Agriculture, Food & Markets
116 State Street, Montpelier, VT 05620
Telephone: 802-828-5667
E-mail: agr-webmaster@state.vt.us
Vermont Seal of Quality
Certified Vermont Made
Telephone: 802-828-3828
In the development and planning stage.

Also check out:

Harvest NE Assoc., Inc.
www.harvestnewengland.org
Agricultural Departments of Connecticut, Maine, Massachusetts, New Hampshire, Rhode Island and Vermont.

Vermont Specialty Food Association
www.vermontspecialtyfoods.org
148 State Street
Montpelier, VT 05602
Telephone: 802-839-1930
E-mail: info@vtspecialtyfoods.org

Virginia
www.vdacs.virginia.gov
Virginia Department of Agriculture and Consumer Services
102 Governor Street, Richmond, Virginia 23219
Telephone: 804-786-3501
Division of Marketing
Telephone: 804-786-3530
Virginia's Finest
www.vafinest.com     www.shopvafinest.com
Telephone: 800-284-9452 / 804-786-4278
In addition to the online services, the VDACS also publishes a Virginia Food and Beverage
Directory that you can get by request.

Washington
www.agr.wa.gov
Washington State Department of Agriculture
Natural Resources Building
1111 Washington Street SE, Olympia, WA 98504-2560
Telephone: 360-902-1800
International Marketing
Telephone: 360-902-1925
From The Heart of Washington
www.heartofwashington.com

Also check out:

Northwest Specialty Foods Association and Agri-Business Council of Oregon
www.nwspecialtyfoods.org
1200 NW Naito Parkway #290, Portland, OR 97209
Telephone: 503-241-1487
Association between Oregon and Washington businesses.

Washington State Food & Agriculture Suppliers
www.impact.wsu.edu/wasuppliers

West Virginia
www.wvagriculture.org
West Virginia Department of Agriculture
1900 Kanawha Boulevard, East, State Capitol, Room E-28, Charleston, WV 25305-0170
Telephone: 304-558-3200
Marketing & Development Division
Telephone: 304-558-2210
West Virginia Grown
www.wvagriculture.org/Foods_and_Things.htm
West Virginia Food & Things Directory - Producer guide and directory

Wisconsin
www.datcp.wi.gov
Wisconsin Department of Agriculture, Trade & Consumer Protection
2811 Agriculture Drive, Madison, WI 53708-8911
Telephone: 608-224-5012
Division of Agricultural Development
Telephone: 608-224-5100
Savor Wisconsin
www.savorwisconsin.com
Telephone: 608-224-5134 / 877-947-6233
E-mail: datcpsavorwisconsin@wisconsin.gov
Managed by WIDATPA, Wisconsin Apple Growers & UW-Extension
Something Special from Wisconsin
www.datcp.state.wi.us/mktg/business/gifts/index.jsp

Wyoming
www.wyagric.state.wy.us/
Wyoming Department of Agriculture
Wyoming First
Telephone: 307-777-2800 / 800-262-3425
E-mail: info@wyo.gov

Also check out:

Wyoming Business Council
www.wyomingbusiness.org
214 West 15th St.
Cheyenne, WY 82002-0204

# 2. State Fair Listings

       Contact your Ag Department about State Fair dates and locations or check the websites below.  There is usually a large display of products at the State Fairs for you to see and taste a multitude of products all in one location.  Local and county fairs are also wonderful opportunities for finding products and talking to the actual product makers.

Alabama State Fair - www.alstatefair.com
       Alabama National Fair - www.alnationalfair.org
Alaska State Fair - www.alaskastatefair.org
       Alaska - Tanana Valley State Fair - www.tananavalleystatefair.com
Arkansas State Fair - www.arkansasstatefair.com
Arizona State Fair - www.azstatefair.com
California State Fair - www.bigfun.org
Colorado State Fair - www.coloradostatefair.com
Connecticut - No State Fair - County Fairs - www.ctagfairs.org
       Connecticut - Durham Fair - www.durhamfair.com
Delaware State Fair - www.delawarestatefair.com
Florida State Fair - www.floridastatefair.com
Georgia State Fair - www.georgiastatefair.org
Hawaii State Farm Fair - www.hfbf.org
Idaho State Fair - Eastern Fair - www.idaho-state-fair.com
Idaho State Fair - Western Fair - www.idahofair.com
Illinois State Fair - www.agr.state.il.us/isf/
Indiana State Fair - www.in.gov/statefair/
Iowa State Fair - www.iowastatefair.org
Kansas State Fair - www.kansasstatefair.com
Kentucky State Fair - www.kystatefair.org
Louisiana State Fair - www.statefairoflouisiana.com
       Louisiana - Greater Baton Rouge State Fair - www.gbrsf.com
Maine - Bangor State Fair - www.bangorstatefair.com
       Maine Association Agricultural Fairs - www.mainefairs.org
Maryland State Fair - www.marylandstatefair.com
Massachusetts State Fair - New England States Fair - www.thebige.com
Michigan - No State Fair
Minnesota State Fair - www.mnstatefair.org
Mississippi State Fair - www.mdac.state.ms.us/departments/ms_fair_commission/index.html
Missouri State Fair - www.mostatefair.com
Montana State Fair - www.montanastatefair.com/index.php
Nebraska State Fair - www.statefair.org
Nevada State Fair - No State Fair
New Hampshire - Hopkinton State Fair - www.hsfair.org

New Jersey State Fair - www.njstatefair.com
New Mexico State Fair - Expo New Mexico - www.exponm.com
New York State Fair - www.nysfair.org
North Carolina State Fair - www.ncstatefair.org
North Dakota State Fair - www.ndstatefair.com
Ohio State Fair - www.ohiostatefair.com
Oklahoma State Fair - www.okstatefair.com
Oregon State Fair - www.oregonstatefair.org
Pennsylvania - No State Fair
      Many Pennsylvania County Fairs - www.pafairs.org
Rhode Island State Fair - No State Fair
      Washington County Fair - www.washingtoncountyfair-ri.com
South Carolina State Fair - www.scstatefair.org
South Dakota State Fair - www.sdstatefair.com
Tennessee State Fair - www.tnstatefair.org
Texas State Fair - www.bigtex.com
      North Texas Fair and Rodeo - www.ntfair.com
      East Texas State Fair - www.etstatefair.com
      Central Texas State Fair - www.centraltexasstatefair.com
Utah State Fair - www.utahstatefair.com
Vermont State Fair - www.vermontstatefair.net
Virginia - No State Fair
Washington - Evergreen State Fair - www.evergreenfair.org
      Central Washington State Fair - www.fairfun.com
West Virginia State Fair - www.wvstatefair.com
Wisconsin State Fair - www.wistatefair.com
Wyoming State Fair - www.wystatefair.com

# 3. The Grocery Store

      I am located Northeast of the Dallas - Fort Worth Metroplex, close enough for convenience, but away from the hassle of the big city. While our selection of stores is limited, we have a family owned chain of grocery stores that cater to our smaller towns.

      As a regional basket owner I especially liked the fact that they would stock new and interesting products from very small manufacturers, usually those just starting out. I tasted a lot of new products. I was always on the lookout for a new salsa or candied jalapeno or even a new chili or bean seasoning. I could purchase one item and go home and try it. In the past I have found literally dozens of start up companies with absolutely wonderful products for my baskets.

      If I was interested in a product and liked the packaging, I would call and request a wholesale catalog and price list from the company. Their address, and sometimes their website, is on the label. If the label reads, "made for..." the company is a reseller and does not actually make the product. I was very careful about this practice and found several companies buying their products out of state and not indicating this on the label. I insisted that our products be made in Texas or they did not go into my baskets, no matter how good they were!

Speak to the store manager directly and introduce yourself and your company. Let them know what products you are interested in and that you would like to purchase in case lots at a discount. Don't pay the shelf price. Ask about their schedule for special orders and when to expect delivery. It is generally cheaper to give them a little more than wholesale if you don't have to pay the freight. This is especially true on heavy items in glass jars like salsa or jelly. It is also more convenient to go to your local grocery store to pick up supplies rather than drive 80 miles round trip to a manufacturer. Price it both ways and use the method best for you.

Placing an order with the grocer also assures you of getting the quantities of the products you need. If you "pop into the grocery store" for supplies, only a limited amount may be on hand at full retail price.

# 4. Gift And Gourmet Shops

Visit gift stores and gourmet shops in your area. What do they have to offer and where are they made? Sometimes the shops have tastings and you can actually sample the products. If they don't, and you find something that looks promising, make the purchase and try it at home. You always want to sample the products before buying a case only to find out that it tastes horrible! The company contact information will be on each label or box.

Sometimes you zero in on a great product that no one else seems to know about. These are the ones that will make your company stand out from the rest.

# 5. Specialty Food Associations

Chocolate and Confectionary Organization
www.candyusa.org/about/members/manufacturers.asp
Great site for manufacturers of jelly beans, taffy, gum, lollipops, cotton candy, gummy and much more.

International Herb Association
www.iherb.org
Searchable companies who grow herbs and make products using herbs.
Excellent product search and product selection.

National Confectioners Association
www.candyusa.com
www.confectioneryandsnacksourcebook.com
Snacks, cookies, candies, supplies, brokers and wholesale.

Specialty Food Association
136 Madison Ave., 12th Floor
New York, NY 10016
Telephone:  212-482-6440
Fax:  212-482-6459

# 6. Warehouse Clubs And Stores

You may think that the large warehouse stores and clubs like Sam's and Costco are your competition, but they aren't.  The gift baskets they offer are mainly packaging and may have been on the shelf for months in anticipation of a certain holiday or season.  You are offering a one of a kind basket with fresh, locally purchased, quality products and plenty of wonderful customer service!

If you are not strict about where your containers are made, these clubs may have inexpensive solutions to save you money.  Go shopping with an open mind - almost anything can be converted into a gift basket container.

# 7. Convention And Market Centers - Trade Shows

Several times a year, usually located in the larger cities, gourmet food shows and gift markets are held in convention and marketing centers.  Manufacturers from all over the country attend these markets to showcase their products to hundred of buyers.

In Dallas we have the World Trade Center, the Trade Mart, Market Hall, etc.  Many manufacturers and reps have showrooms open throughout the year to buyers while others lease space only during a major show or event.  Other major markets are in Chicago, New York and California.  If you can't attend one of the major trade shows, check the event website or call the organizer and request a list of attending companies.  Use this information to contact those from your state.

The permanent market locations, like the Dallas Trade Mart, print a Market Vendor Book which lists the companies that have year round showrooms.  The market and show schedule should also be in the book and on the website.  You must be registered as a buyer in advance to attend the shows.  Contact the trade centers for registration requirements several weeks prior to any event you want to attend.

The following list of convention centers, trade centers and markets is a good source for product manufacturers.  Contact your local Chamber of Commerce or Convention and Visitors Bureau for events scheduled in your local area and registration requirements.

Convention Center Directories:
CVent Destination Guide - Convention Center Directory
http://www.cvent.com/rfp/us-convention-centers-50e04fe6bd5e4dffbd1bebd80ea83db7.aspx

Convention Center Directory
http://conventioncenterdirectory.com/

Alabama
Birmingham-Jefferson Convention Center
www.bjcc.org
2100 Richard Arrington, Jr. Blvd. North, Birmingham, AL 35217
Telephone: 205-458-8400


Alaska
Egan Civic And Convention Center
www.anchorageconventioncenters.com/egan-center/
555 W. Fifth Ave., Anchorage, AK 99501
Telephone: 907-263-2800

Dena'ina Civic and Convention Center
http://www.anchorageconventioncenters.com/denaina-center/
600 W. Seventh Ave., Anchorage, AK 99501
Telephone: 907-263-2850

Centennial Hall Convention Center
www.juneau.org/centennial/
101 Egam Drive, Juneau, AK 99801
Telephone: 907-586-5283


Arizona
Tucson Convention Center
www.tucsonaz.gov/tcc
260 South Church Ave., Tucson, AZ 85701
Telephone: 520-791-4101


Arkansas
Fort Smith Convention Center
www.fortsmithar.gov/conventioncenter/default.aspx
55 South 7th Street, Ft. Smith, AR 72901
Telephone: 479-788-8932


California
California Market Center
www.californiamarketcenter.com
110 East Ninth St., Los Angeles, CA 90079
Telephone: 213-630-3600

Los Angeles Convention Center
www.lacclink.com
1201 S. Figueroa St., Los Angeles, CA 90015
Telephone: 213-741-1151 / 800-448-7775

Moscone Center
www.moscone.com
747 Howard St., San Francisco, CA 94103
Telephone: 415-974-4000

The LA Mart
www.lamart.com
1933 South Broadway, Los Angeles, CA 90007
Telephone: 800-526-2784
E-mail: info@lamart.com

Colorado
Denver Merchandise Mart
www.denvermart.com
451 E. 58th Ave., Suite 470, Denver, CO 80216
Telephone: 303-292-6278 / 800-292-6278
E-mail: info@denvermart.com

Connecticut
Connecticut Convention Center
www.ctconventions.com
100 Columbus Blvd., Hartford, CT 06103
Telephone: 860-249-6000

Delaware
Chase Center
www.centerontheriverfront.com
815 Justison St., Wilmington, DE 19801
Telephone: 888-862-2787

Rehoboth Beach Convention Center
www.cityofrehoboth.com
229 Rehoboth Ave., Rehoboth Beach, DE 19971
Telephone: 302-227-4641

Florida
Emerald Coast Convention Center
www.emeraldcoastconventioncenter.com
1250 Miracle Strip Pkwy. SE, Ft. Walton Beach, FL 32548
Telephone: 850-609-3800

Miami International Merchandise Mart
www.miamimerchantmart.com
777 N.W. 72nd Ave., Miami, FL 33126
Telephone: 305-269-4811
E-mail: info@miamimerchantmart.com

Orange County Convention Center
www.occc.net
9800 International Drive, Orlando, FL 32819
Telephone: 407-685-9800
E-mail: info@occc.net

Georgia
AmericasMart Atlanta
www.americasmart.com
240 Peachtree St. NW, Suite 2200, Atlanta, GA 30303-1327
Telephone: 800-285-6278

Hawaii
Blaisdell Exhibition Center
www.blaisdellcenter.com
777 Ward Ave., Honolulu, HI 96814
Telephone: 808-768-5400 / 800-525-5275

Hawaii Convention Center
www.hawaiiconvention.com
1801 Kalakaua Ave., Honolulu, Hawaii 96815
Telephone: 808-943-3500 / 800-295-6603

Idaho
Boise Convention Centre
www.boisecentre.com
850 W. Front Street, Boise, ID 83702
Telephone: 208-336-8900

Illinois
Donald E. Stephens Convention Center
www.rosemont.com
5555 N. River Rd., Rosemont, IL 60018
Telephone: 847-692-2220 / 847-692-2222

Gateway Convention Center
www.gatewaycenter.com
One Gateway Drive, Collinsville, IL 62234
Telephone: 618-345-8998 / 800-289-2388
E-mail: info@gatewaycenter.com

McCormick Place
www.mccormickplace.com
2301 S. Lake Shore Drive, Chicago, IL 60616
Telephone: 312-791-7000

The Chicago Market
www.shopchicagomarket.com
www.mmart.com

The Merchandise Mart
www.mmart.com
222 Merchandise Mart Plaza, Chicago, IL 60654
Telephone: 312-527-3332 / 800-677-6278

Indiana
Allen County War Memorial Coliseum
www.memorialcoliseum.com
4000 Parnell Ave., Ft. Wayne, Indiana 46805
Telephone: 260-482-9502

Iowa
Iowa Events Center
www.iowaeventscenter.com
730 Third Street, Des Moines, IA 50309
Telephone: 515-564-8000

Kansas
Gift Mart of Kansas City
www.giftmartofkansascity.com
9541A Metcalf Ave., Overland Park, KS 66212
Telephone: 913-687-8059

Overland Park Convention Center
www.opconventioncenter.com
6000 College Blvd., Overland Park, KS  66211
Telephone:  913-339-3000

Overland Park International Trade Center
www.optradecenter.com
6800 W. 115th Street, Overland Park, KS  66211
Telephone:  913-451-7691


Kentucky
Kentucky Crafted:  The Market
www.state.ky.us/agencies/crafts/crafthome.htm
www.kycraft.ky.gov
Kentucky Fair and Exposition Center - Wing B
Telephone:  502-564-3757 / 888-592-7238

Kentucky International Convention Center
www.kyconvention.org
221 4th Street, Louisville, KY  40202
Telephone:  502-595-4381 / 800-701-5831

Lexington Convention Center
www.lexingtoncenter.com/lexington-convention-center
430 W. Vine Street, Lexington, KY  40507
Telephone:  859-233-4567

Paroquet Conference Centre
www.paroquetsprings.org
395 Paroquet Springs Drive, Shepherdsville, KY  40165
Telephone - 502-955-7009


Louisiana
Morial Convention Center
www.mccno.com
900 Convention Center Blvd., New Orleans, LA  70130
Telephone:  504-582-3000
E-mail:  m-s@mccno.com

Maine
Cumberland County Civic Center
www.theciviccenter.com
One Civic Center Square, Portland, ME 04101
Telephone: 207-775-3458


Maryland
Baltimore Convention Center
www.bccenter.org
One West Pratt Street, Baltimore, MD 21201
Telephone: 410-649-7000

Roland E. Powell Convention Center
www.ococean.com
4001 Coastal Highway, Ocean City, MD 21842
Telephone: 410-289-2800 / 800-626-2326
E-mail: ask@ococean.com


Massachusetts
Best Western Royal Plaza Hotel & Trade Center
www.rplazahotels.com/trade-center.htm
181 Boston Post Road W., Marlborough, MA 01752
Telephone: 888-543-9500

Boston Convention & Exhibition Center
www.massconvention.com
415 Summer Street, Boston, MA 02210
Telephone: 617-954-2000

John B. Hynes Veterans Memorial Convention Center
www.massconvention.com
900 Boyston Street, Boston, MA 02115
Telephone: 617-954-2000

MassMutual Convention Center
www.massmutualcenter.com
1277 Main Street, Springfield, MA 01103
Telephone: 413-787-6610

North East Market Center
www.northeastmarketcenter.com
2 Cabot Road, Hudson, MA  01749
Telephone:  800-435-2775
E-mail:  info@northeastmarketcenter.com

Michigan
The Lansing Conventional Center
www.lepfa.com
333 E. Michigan Avenue, Lansing, MI  48933
Telephone:  517-483-7400

Minnesota
Minneapolis Mart
www.mplsmart.com
10301 Bren Road West, Minnetonka, MN  55343
Telephone:  952-932-7200 / 800-626-1298

Mississippi
Mississippi Coast Coliseum and Convention Center
www.mscoastcoliseum.com
2350 Beach Blvd., Biloxi, MS  39531
Telephone:  228-594-3700 / 800-726-2781

Mississippi Trade Mart
www.mdac.state.ms.us/departments/ms_fair_commission/fg-trademart.htm
1200 E. Mississippi Street, Jackson, MS  39202
Telephone:  601-354-7051 / 800-951-1994
The Mississippi Development Authority sponsors the Mississippi Market each year.
www.mississippimarket.org
Telephone:  888-886-3323

Missouri
St. Charles Convention Center
www.stcharlesconventioncenter.com
One Convention Center Plaza, St. Charles, MO  63303
Telephone:  636-669-3000

Montana
Billings, Montana Convention Center
www.higrandmt.com
Holiday Inn Grand Montana, 5500 Midland Rd., Billings, MT  59101
Telephone:  406-248-7701

Nebraska
Grow Nebraska
www.grownebraska.org
PO Box 7, Holbrook, NE  68948
Telephone:  888-476-9632
E-mail:  info@grownebraska.org

Nevada
Las Vegas Convention Center
www.vegasmeansbusiness.com
3150 Paradise Road, Las Vegas, NV  89109
Telephone:  702-892-0711 / 877-847-4858

Mandalay Bay Resort and Casino
www.mandalaybay.com
3950 Las Vegas Blvd. South, Las Vegas, NV  89119
Telephone:  702-632-7777 / 877-632-7900

Sands Expo Convention Center
www.sandsexpo.com
201 Sands Ave., Las Vegas, NV  89109
Telephone:  702-733-5556

World Market Center Las Vegas
www.lasvegasmarket.com
495 S. Grand Central Pkwy., Las Vegas, NV  89106
Telephone:  702-599-9621 / 888-416-8600
E-mail:  info@imcenters.com

New Hampshire
Radisson Hotel Expo Center of New Hampshire
www.radisson.com/manchesternh
700 Elm Street, Manchester, NH  03101
Telephone:  603-625-1000

New Jersey
Atlantic City Convention Center
www.accenter.com
One Convention Blvd., Atlantic City, NJ  08401
Telephone:  609-449-2000 / 888-222-3683
E-mail:  info@accenter.com

New Jersey Convention & Exhibition Center
www.njexpocenter.com
97 Sunfield Ave., Edison, NJ 08837
Telephone: 732-417-1400
E-mail: info@njexpocenter.com


New York
Jacob K. Javits Convention Center
www.javitscenter.com
655 West 34th Street, New York, NY 10001
Telephone: 212-216-2000
E-mail: moreinfo@javitscenter.com

New York Market Center
www.230fifthavenue.com
230 Fifth Ave., New York, NY 10010
Telephone: 800-698-5617

7 West 34th New York
www.7wnewyork.com
7 West 34th Street, New York, NY 10001
Telephone: 646.778.3200 / 800 677 6278

The New York Merchandise Mart
www.41madison.com
Forty One Madison Ave., New York, NY 10010
Telephone: 212-686-1203


North Carolina
The Park Expo and Conference Center
www.ppm-nc.com
800 Briar Creek Road, Charlotte, NC 28205
Telephone: 704-333-7709


Ohio
Columbus Marketplace For Gift, Garden and Home
www.thecolumbusmarketplace.com
7001 Discovery Blvd., Dublin, OH 43017
Telephone: 614-339-5100 / 888-332-8979

Franklin County Veterans Memorial Bldg.
www.fcvm.com
300 West Broad Street, Columbus, OH  43215
Telephone:  614-221-4341
E-mail:  info@fcvm.com

The Ohio Expo Center and State Fair
www.expo.state.oh.us
717 East 17th Avenue, Columbus, OH  43211
Telephone:  614-644-3247 / 888-OHO-EXPO
E-mail: info@expo.state.oh.us

Oklahoma
Cox Convention Center
www.coxconventioncenter.com
1 Myriad Gardens, Oklahoma City, OK  73102-9219
Telephone:  405-602-8500 / 800-951-1994

Oregon
Oregon Convention Center
www.oregoncc.org
777 NE Martin Luther King, Jr. Blvd., Portland, OR  97232
Telephone:  503-235-7575 / 800-791-2251

Pennsylvania
Pennsylvania Convention Center
www.paconvention.com
1101 Arch St., Philadelphia, PA  19107
Telephone:  215-418-4700 / 800-428-9000

Monroeville Convention Center
www.monroevilleconventioncenter.com
209 Mall Blvd., Monroeville, PA  15146
Telephone:  412-373-7300

Valley Forge Convention Center
www.vfconventioncenter.com
1160 First Ave., King of Prussia, PA  19406
Telephone:  610-768-3215

Eisenhower Hotel and Conference Center
www.eisenhower.com
2634 Emmetsburg Rd., Gettysburg, PA 17325
Telephone: 717-334-8121

Rhode Island
Rhode Island Convention Center
www.riconvention.com
One Salem Street, Providence, RI 02903
Telephone: 401-458-6000

South Carolina
Myrtle Beach Convention Center
www.myrtlebeachconventioncenter.com
2101 North Oak Street, Myrtle Beach, SC 29578
Telephone: 843-918-1225 / 800-537-1690

South Dakota
Sioux Falls Convention Center
www.sfarena.com/sioux_falls_convention_center
1101 N. West Ave., Sioux Falls, SD 57104
Telephone: 605-367-4167

Tennessee
Gatlinburg Convention Center
www.meetings.gatlinburg.com/meet/convention-center
234 Historic Nature Trail, Gatlinburg, TN 37738
Telephone: 865-277-8967

Memphis-Cook Convention Center
www.memphistravel.com/conventions/memphis-cook-center
255 North Main St., Memphis, TN 38103
Telephone: 901-576-1200

Nashville Convention Center
www.nashvilleconventionctr.com
601 Commerce, Nashville, TN 37203
Telephone: 615-742-2000

Sevierville Convention Center
www.seviervilleeventscenter.com
202 Gists Creek Rd., Sevierville, TN 37876
Telephone: 865-453-0001

Texas
Austin Convention Center
www.austinconventioncenter.com
500 E. Cesar Chavez St., Austin, TX  78701
Telephone:  512-404-4000

Dallas Market Center
www.dallasmarketcenter.com
2100 Stemmons Freeway, Dallas, Texas  75207
Telephone:  214-655-6100 / 214-744-7444 / 800-325-6587

Galveston Island Convention Center
www.galvestonislandconventioncenter.com
5600 Seawall Blvd., Galveston, TX  77550
Telephone:  866-505-4456


Utah
South Towne Exposition Centre
www.southtowneexpo.com
9575 S. State Street, Sandy, UT  84070
Telephone:  385-468-2260


Vermont
Champlain Valley Exposition
www.cvexpo.org
105 Pearl Street, Essex Junction, VT  05453
Telephone:  802-878-5545


Virginia
Dulles Expo and Conference Center
www.dullesexpo.com
4320 Chantilly Shopping Center, Chantilly, VA  20153
Telephone:  703-378-0910

Virginia Beach Convention Center
www.visitvirginiabeach.com/conventioncenter/
1000  19th Street, Virginia Beach, VA  23451
Telephone:  757-385-2000
E-Mail:  vbcc@vbgov.com

Washington
Pacific Market Center
www.pacmarket.com
6100 4th Ave. South, Seattle, WA 98108
Telephone: 206-767-6800 / 800-433-1014
E-mail: Info@pacmarket.com

Washington State Convention Center
www.wscc.com
800 Convention Place, Seattle, WA 98101
Telephone: 206-694-5000
E-mail: info@wscc.com

West Virginia
Charleston Civic Center
www.charlestonwvciviccenter.com
200 Civic Center Drive, Charleston, WV 25301
Telephone: 304-345-1500

Wisconsin
Alliant Energy Center, Exhibition Hall
www.alliantenergycenter.com
1919 Alliant Energy Center Way, Madison, WI 53713
Telephone: 608-267-3976

Wyoming
Casper Events Center
www.caspereventscenter.com
#1 Events Drive, Casper, WY 82601
Telephone: 307-577-3030 / 800-442-2256

# 8. Management Groups / Association Trade Shows

The following management companies and associations operate buyer's shows in numerous cities across the USA. Check their websites for show schedules and locations.

ASD - www.asdonline.com - 800-421-4511

Coral Productions - www.coralproductions.com - 585-254-2580

Douglas Trade Shows - www.douglastradeshows.com
        808-254-1773 / 800-525-5275    Trade shows in Hawaii.

EventPros - www.eventprosinc.com - 816-960-3400

Expo Promotion - www.lansinggiftshow.com / www.nmgiftshow.com - 231-526-1270

Family Festivals Association - www.familyfestivals.com - 724-863-4577

GLM Shows - www.glmshows.com - 800-292-4560
Produces 22 trade shows including the National Stationery Show

Great Rep, LLC - www.greatrep.com
Internet directory of the wholesale giftware industry - listings of wholesale trade gift shows.

H.H. Backer Associates, Inc. - www.hhbacker.com - 312-578-1818
Pet Industry trade show.

Kentucky Arts Council - www.kycraft.ky.gov - 501-564-3757 / 888-833-2787
State agency sponsored shows for the arts and craft businesses in Kentucky.

Market Square Association - www.marketsquareshows.com - 717-796-2377 / 570-873-3054

Norton Shows - www.nortonshows.com - 865-436-6151

OASIS, Inc. - www.oasis.org - 602-952-2050 / 800-424-9619

Offinger's Marketplaces - www.offinger.com - 888-878-4438

Progressive Exhibitors, Inc. - 801-782-7771

Rosehill Enterprises, Inc. - www.rosehillenterprisesinc.com - 513-861-1139

Specialty Food Association, Inc. - www.specialtyfood.com - 212-482-6440
Fancy Food Shows

The National Gift Basket Convention - www.thengbc.com - 877-491-8729

Urban Exposition - www.urban-expo.com - 800-318-2238

Western Exhibitors - www.weshows.com - 415-346-6666

Wholesale Markets, Inc. - www.wmigiftshows.com - 405-373-2020 / 800-951-1994

# 9. Trade Magazines And More

Fancy Food & Culinary Products Magazine
www.fancyfoodmagazine.com
Telephone: 312-849-2220
Digital magazine.

Florist Review Magazine
www.floristsreview.com
Telephone: 800-367-4708
Wholesale florists listed by state. Predominately for florists but the gift basket designer can pick up great tips from the site. How-to-info on the site. "Source Book" for gift baskets, ribbon, containers, specialty and gourmet foods, etc.

Gift Basket Review Online
www.festivities-pub.com
Online gift basket magazine with articles, videos, etc. Several free design ideas and product supplier list. Annual subscription fee for the magazine.

Gift Biz Buzz
www.giftbizbuzz.com
Online trade magazine featuring new product information for gift retailers.

Gift, Gourmet and Decor
www.ggdplus.com
Digital Magazine - product e-catalogs on their site.

Gift Shop Magazine
www.giftshopmag.com
Telephone: 800-936-6297
Articles online to help the gift basket professional and other gift retailers. Print magazine and digital magazine subscriptions available.

Gifts & Decorative Accessories
www.giftsanddec.com
Telephone: 800-309-3332
Has a searchable market calendar by city and state online. Also, gift product listings.

Giftware News Magazine
www.giftwarenewsmagazine.com
Telephone: 312-849-2220

Green Retailer
www.giftshopmag.com/green_retailer
Same publisher as Gift Shop Magazine.  Specializes in Eco-Friendly resources for the retailer.

Gourmet Retailer
www.gourmetretailer.com
Telephone:  224-632-8200
A buyers guide is located under the resource section with gourmet food company listings.  Search by state.

Party & Paper Retailer
www.partypaper.com
Telephone:  616-887-9008
Digital and print magazine.  Online sourcebook with many suppliers listed.

Smart Retailer
www.smart-retailer.com
Telephone:  630-377-8000  /  888-228-7624
For gift retailers - includes a new product showcase.

# 10. Associations

American Craft Council
www.craftcouncil.org
1224 Marshal St. NE, #200, Minneapolis, MN  55413
Telephone:  612-206-3100 / 800-836-3470
Several shows of handcrafted items and artist's works.

Art Glass Suppliers Association
www.artglassassociation.info
5610 Pleasant View Drive, Nashport, OH  43830
Telephone:  740-450-6547 / 866-301-2421

Craft & Hobby Association
www.craftandhobby.org   and  www.craftplace.org
319 E. 54th St., Elmwood Park, NJ  07407
Telephone:  201-835-1200
Trade shows and information.

Gift Retailers Connection
www.giftretailersconnection.com
Download a free magazine.  Subscribers to the magazine receive a monthly newsletter, access to their forum and a text listing for their company in the directory.

Indian Arts & Crafts Association
www.iaca.com
4010 Carlisle Blvd. NE, Suite C, Albuquerque, NM  87107
Telephone:  505-265-9149
Trade shows and seminars.

International Housewares Association
www.housewares.org
6400 Shafer Court, Suite 650, Rosemont, IL  60018
Telephone:  847-292-4200 /  800-752-1052
International Home and Housewares show.
Directory of housewares companies:  www.housewares.org/housewaresconnect365/?
The directory is searchable by state, Made in America and more.

National Association of Miniature Enthusiasts
www.miniatures.org
Telephone:  317-571-8094
Conventions, shows and events.

National Candle Association
www.candles.org
529  14th St. NW, #750, Washington, DC  20045
Telephone:  202-591-2455
Search for suppliers and manufacturers:
www.candles.org/NCA_suppliers.html
www.candles.org/NCA_manufacturers.html

The Gift and Home Trade Association
www.giftandhome.org
2550 Sandy Plains Rd., Suite 225, Marietta, GA  30066
Telephone:  877-600-4872

The Gift Basket Association
www.giftbasketassociation.com
Membership and listing on www.findyourgiftbasket.com for $10.00 per month

The Specialty Food Trade Association
www.specialtyfood.com          www.specialtyfoodmagazine.com
120 Wall Street, 27th Floor, New York, NY  10005
Holds the Fancy Food Shows.  Membership to join but you can search for products online for free.
The website showcases new products each month.

The Toy Industry Association, Inc.
www.toyinfo.org
1115 Broadway, Suite 400, New York, NY  10010
Telephone:  212-675-1141
Trade association for businesses involved in creating toys and entertainment products.  Member
directory and search by state.

Western Toy & Hobby Representatives Association
www.wthra.com          www.toyfestwest.com
Telephone:  909-899-3753

Wholesale Crafts
www.wholesalecrafts.com
PO Box 4597, Mooresville, NC  28117-4597 / 888-427-2381
1200 wholesale artists and online marketplace.

Wholesale Florist and Florist Supplier Association
www.wffsa.org
Find a wholesale florist - has a search function on the website.
www.wffsa.org/aws/wffsa/pt/sp/directory_public
Telephone:  410-940-6580 / 888-289-3372


# 11. The Yellow Pages

The local yellow pages, or internet yellow pages, is a great reference to locate local food
manufacturers, suppliers of floral items and even basket or tray makers.

Floral wholesale suppliers carry all sorts of picks, cards, teddy bears, coffee mugs, etc., to
embellish your baskets and should know which items are made in your state.

A resale certificate is generally needed to shop with these wholesale suppliers.  Remember to
ask about initial order and reorder amount minimums.

# 12. Gift Basket Supply Companies

If you can't locate your products locally, contact the companies listed in this section. You will have to register with these companies and prove you are a retailer or wholesale customer. Most only need a State Resale Tax ID or a DBA Certificate.

When you call, ask them:

1) Do they warehouse the items or send your order directly to the manufacturer?

2) Do they guarantee their products to be fresh and for how long?

3) What are their initial order minimums and reorder minimums?

4) Do they have quantity discounts or specials?

5) How quickly can they get an order processed and to you?

6) Do they pay the freight if you purchase a certain amount?

7) Do they use a shipping company that is reliable?

8) Do they have a toll free number for ordering and customer service?

9) What are their hours of operation? Open on Saturday?

10) Do they offer no hassle returns?

11) Can you get samples, or purchase individual items, prior to ordering?

All Sorts Premium Packaging - www.clearcandybags.com - 888-565-9727
    Bags, cello, containers, ribbon, shred and more.

Gift Basket Suppliers - www.giftbasketsuppliers.com -
    They don't sell products but have a great online data base directory, list of trade shows, suppliers, gift baskets companies, food & packaging supplies, suppliers and even web hosting companies.

Gift Baskets Supplies - www.giftbasketsupplies.com - 714-634-3478
    Mostly food products and some packaging.

Gift Basket Wholesale Supply - www.giftbasketwholesalesupply.com - 888-601-3064
    A directory of wholesale suppliers for gift basket designers. Also has newsletters, tips and suggestions and even instructions on making a gift basket from start to finish.

<u>Gourmet Products, Inc.</u> - www.gourmetproductsinc.com - 800-541-2215

This is a great company representing some excellent product manufacturers. The orders are sent directly to the manufacturers assuring you of fresh products for your baskets. Just let them know where you are located and ask if they have manufacturers they represent from your state. The wholesale prices through this company are the same as through the manufacturer directly. With one call you have access to great products, saving you valuable time not having to call 4 or 5 separate companies. They offer exceptional customer service and excellent delivery time. If I sound a little biased, I am. It was the owner of the company, Ann, who held my hand when I first started my company and she was the one who calmed me down during many of my Christmas emergencies! Give them a call or check out the website.

If you can not locate a basket manufacturer in your state, GPI represents Vinetiques. They manufacture baskets in the shape of the states and many more styles that you might like. Vinetique has excellent products and customer service as well. Access their products through the GPI website.

<u>MAC Paper Supply, Inc.</u> - www.Macpaper.com - 800-486-5788

Wholesale gift packaging.

<u>National Specialty Gift Association</u> - www.nsgaonline.com - 813-374-1777

A directory of wholesale suppliers for gift basket designers, newsletters, tips and suggestions. Instructions and videos on making a gift basket, classes and workshops.

A vendor directory: www.nsgaonline.com/directory/index.html

<u>Nashville Wraps</u> - www.nashvillewraps.com - 800-547-9727

Carries a nice selection of ribbon and bows, gift cards, rolled paper, holders, tape and tape dispensers, and much more. I used Nashville Wraps if I could not get my supplies locally. Excellent delivery times, product selection and their prices are great. Free "how to" videos demonstrating how to put a basket together, wrap a gift basket and various shrink wrap techniques.

<u>Papermart</u> - www.Papermart.com - 800-745-8800

Packaging, shreds, gift packaging and boxes.

<u>Premier Packaging</u> - www.retailpackaging.com - 800-203-5558

No minimum order but does charge a handling fee.

<u>ULINE</u> - www.uline.com - 800-295-5510

Shipping supply specialists. Boxes, bubble, paper and peanuts are only some of their products. Locations in Chicago, Minneapolis, Dallas, Atlanta, Los Angeles, Seattle and NYC/ Philadelphia. Offers next day delivery.

# 13. Thomas Registry

A HUGE set of books that tells you who makes what, and where, in the USA. Find these books in the library's reference section or on the internet at www.thomasnet.com.

For example, you can look under pencils and then under your state and find a manufacturer with their contact information. Thomas Registry provides a distinct advantage to you if you are looking to purchase directly from the maker of your products and not through a third party. Contact the company directly to find out their purchasing requirements. If they only sell through their representatives, they will give you their contact information. When you find a product you are interested in, be sure to ask if it is made in your state. Many manufacturers today are producing products overseas and only warehousing their products for distribution here in the US

# Chapter 4
# Contacting Your Suppliers

Now that you know who makes the products you need for your baskets, contact the manufacturers, identify yourself as the owner of XYZ Basket Company and tell them you would like information on their products. If you are only interested in one or two of their products, when you request information on those specific items they may offer to send you samples. If they don't offer, ask for samples. Most companies will send you one or two items, but not all 53 products they offer! Also, when you deal directly with the manufacturer, they will notify you of new products, special sales and promotions.

When you consider products for your baskets, ask questions:

1) What is the shelf life of the product? Look for products that will last a year or longer. This won't apply to items like handmade candies, etc., but will apply to your seasonings, soup mixes, salsas & dips, etc.

2) Will it last longer if refrigerated? The shelf life of some items can be extended by refrigeration. Pralines that last 60 days in a cool room might last 90 days or longer if stored in the refrigerator.

3) Can the items be frozen? When I ordered pecans it was always a large order and I would put the pecan packages in gallon zip lock bags in the freezer. Pecans will keep up to a year in the freezer. Great tactic if you over purchased at Christmas. Some foods, like chocolate, change color and while the taste isn't affected the product no longer looks very appetizing in your basket. If you

freeze something, let it come to room temperature before adding it to your wrapped basket to prevent sweating.

4) How much am I required to purchase at a time? Some manufacturers will sell you one jar if you pick it up at their location. Others want you to buy a minimum of 20 cases before they will ship to you.

5) Is there a minimum dollar amount that I have to spend on each order? Generally the smaller companies will sell you smaller quantities and will work with your needs. Others might require a $200 initial order and every re-order must be at least $50, for example.

6) If you are talking to product reps, do they buy the products and put them in a warehouse or are the orders shipped to you directly from the product manufacturers? Dealing with a company rep can be a great way to go if they send your order to the manufacturer, assuring you of the freshest products. Be cautious when ordering from a warehouse type wholesaler. Occasionally the products are not rotated and stale products get shipped. Pay close attention to the product expiration date when your products arrive and send old products back immediately.

7) What kind of guarantee do you offer? Every once in a while you will run across a jar that did not seal or a seam on a package that didn't quite close. A quick, polite call to the manufacturer will usually get you replacement items or credit on your next order. Call as soon as you know something is wrong. Check every box of inventory when it arrives for the proper count and to be sure everything is ok.

8) Will they send free samples? Can you buy samples if they don't? I can't tell you how many products we have tested over the years. Most were excellent but some were -- shall I say, unacceptable. Even if you have to purchase an item or two, it is better that buying several cases of an item that it is not up to your standards or is really terrible.

9) How long does it take to get an order out? If the factory is constantly running two weeks behind, you need to know so you can plan ahead. If the factory keeps most of their items in stock, they can ship out immediately. This is good to know especially when that big custom order comes in or Christmas orders are coming in faster than you expected and you need supplies fast.

10) How do you ship? After a while you will have a preference as to the delivery service that brings your supplies. If the manufacturer absolutely insists on using a company that consistently loses or delays your supplies, perhaps you shouldn't do business with them.

11) Do you take checks or credit cards and which ones do you honor? Get into the habit of paying by check or business credit card at the time that you place your order. Attach all of the orders together and keep a running total so you know how much is due on your credit card. Some companies will let you pay in 30 days if you fill out a credit application, but I would advise against this. Just as you expect payment from your customers when they order, you should pay your suppliers when placing your orders.

# Chapter 5

# Organizing Your Workspace

<u>Setting up your space:</u>  Depending on whether you are working in a spare bedroom or in the garage, hopefully you will have room to spread out and work comfortably.  There is nothing more aggravating than completing the baskets in one room, moving to the office to type an invoice and shipping label, going to the garage for a box and bubble, taking everything to the middle of the living room floor to pack the gift and finally putting the box at the front door for pickup!  This procedure will cost you time and when you get busy, will make you want to pull your hair out!  If you are only doing an occasional basket, it is not too bad and it will suffice until you can afford more comfortable accommodations.

Treat your new venture as a serious business, not just a hobby.  Organization is the key to being more productive.  Here are a few suggestions:

1) The space should be climate controlled.  Frozen products in glass jars explode and heat causes chocolate to melt and seals to pop.

2) The area should be a non-smoking area.

3) No pets, puppies or kittens.  Shrink wrap is notorious for collecting dust and hair.

4) Bug free and Bug Spray Free! Use non-toxic glue traps if needed.

5) No scents!  Air fresheners, candles, cat boxes, exhaust, etc.will filter into your products. Do not have anything that smells around your food.

The following suggestions would make the ideal situation.  You may not be able to accomplish this from day one, but use the layout as a guideline.  Before you receive your first shipment of products you need to have your space well organized.  A room or a garage space about 20 X 20 would be perfect.  Along one wall put your desk, file cabinet, printer, telephone & fax.

<u>Product Storage:</u>  On one side of the room would be a wall of shelving for your products. Five shelf shelving works great.  I suggest not unloading all of your boxes, but using them to organize.  Take your products out of the box, cut off the top of the boxes and about half of the front to expose the products and then reload the box.

Most of my glass products came in boxes with dividers and my shelves were spaced so I had plenty of room to extract a product from its box without being cramped by the shelf above.   The product boxes should be on one of three shelves that are at waist high level, just above that and just below.  Heavy glass jars should always go close to the floor with the lighter boxes being put on the upper shelves.  The fewer bends that you have to make, the better. On the very top and bottom shelves, put unopened and uncut product cases.

When you receive your products, open every box in the shipment and check the condition of the products. If the product is in sealed glass jars, touch each one of the jar lids to be sure the seal is unbroken. Sometimes just the transporting of jars will break the seal. If something is damaged or broken, let your supplier know immediately.

Check the expiration date on the products. Sometimes you receive products that should be good for 18 months that will expire in only 3 months. Contact the supplier and ask for a replacement. If they do not replace the product at no charge, use the product immediately and get a new supplier. There are plenty of suppliers that would be happy to get your business!

Any unopened boxes on the shelves should be labeled with a felt marker on the exposed end of each box. Write what is in the box, the date you received the product and the expiration date of the product inside. This makes it easy to see which box to use next when you get busy. Always use the oldest one first or the one whose expiration date is the nearest.

Basket Storage: Our working stock was stored on the floor in stacks in an area about 5 X 3 feet. The surplus was kept in the original cartons in a storage area. When I first started I had all sorts of basket shapes, but finally narrowed our selection to only flat tray type baskets. For us these were easier to store, easier to wrap and to ship. This would also work for baskets with smaller handles on both sides that can be nested or stacked. Baskets with the large loop handles are going to take up more room and can not be neatly stacked.

While I have never used this method, some designers use a light rope hanging from the ceiling to the floor and clothes pins or alligator clips to attach the baskets up and down the rope. A light chain and S-Hooks might work better. You may need to experiment with what works best for you, just be sure the rope or chain is securely attached or it could come tumbling down at a most inopportune time!

Assembly and Shrinking Station: A table about 24 - 30 inches wide and about 6 feet long will do nicely to accommodate your shrink wrap machine and your turntable. Put the work table in an open area of the room. You should be able to walk all around the table and it should be close to the product shelves.

My table was made using a 6 foot laminate counter top I purchased at the hardware store. Use a small towel or a piece of thick material about 18X 18 inches under your baskets. I found that by doing this, I could slide even the heaviest of baskets around for sealing without lifting them. You may want to use a turntable to assemble your products. I found the turntable to be aggravating in the assembly process because it would spin just as I was trying to make my final adjustments. Use the turntable in the center of your table to shrink wrap your basket.

On the other end of your assembly table, a desk drawer organizer with compartments works well to keep a supply of pens, scissors, gift cards, business cards and labels organized.

A heavy desktop 2 inch tape dispenser and a smaller scotch tape dispenser should also be on your table near your ribbon and supply organizer.

Your box of shred should be beside your table. A trash can for remnants can go under the table. Use an empty product box for trash and when it gets full, just close the box and put it out for pickup.

Ribbon Storage: If you are using ribbon on a spool, this can get to be a mess in a hurry! Try these ideas to keep the ribbon organized: 1) If you are only using a couple of colors, use a free standing paper towel holder, the kind with a smooth wooden dowel. These will usually hold 3 larger spools and won't take up much table room.  2) You can also use a shoe box.  Put your ribbon in the box and cut a hole in the lid for the ribbon to be pulled through.  Since you can't see through the lid it is easy to run out before you realize it.  There is a clear plastic box made for ribbon storage and this would allow you to see your supply.

Boxes: An area 3 X 5 feet should be reserved for your boxes.  Folded flat they store well on their sides propped against the side of your shelving.  Work on your box sizes until you only need 3 or 4 sizes of boxes.  It makes life easier to have one box that can be used to ship several different baskets.

Paper:  The clean newspaper comes in 50# flat packages.  We made a small stand about 2 foot tall that had a 1 inch dowel across the top.  The paper draped across the dowel which made it very handy when we were packing.  If you put too much paper on the dowel, it will slip off and onto the floor.

Bubble Wrap:  The bubble wrap can be left on the floor if you have room.  A 250 foot roll is about 3.5 - 4 foot in diameter, and can be unrolled and ripped off as needed.  There are commercial holders or you can make your own.  We used a 1 inch dowel rod through the center of the bubble and suspended it from two light weight chains attached to the ceiling. The good thing about the bubble wrap is that it is light.  If you suspend it, you can put your packaging paper and boxes under it for easy access.

Wrapping Station:  The boxes, bubble and packing should be easily accessible to another table for easy assembly.  One year I used a 6 foot plastic folding picnic table with attached benches and it was a joy!  I would lay the bubble on the table to wrap my baskets and then assemble the box on the lower side bench.  Since the side of the box was up against the table top, I could push the lid closed without any help while I taped it shut.  Both sides of the picnic table can be used by several people without getting into anyone's way.  The table also held my tape, tags and supplies.

Shipping Holding Area:  You should have two separate areas for boxes ready to be shipped.  One area should be for the boxes going out today and a separate area for those boxes being held for a future ship out day.

During the holidays customers may need their gift to go out on a certain day.  We had a second holding area for these boxes with a separate stack for each day of the week that these needed to be shipped out.

# Chapter 6
## Pricing Your Baskets

I believe the hardest part of establishing my business was pricing my baskets.

I knew exactly how much each item in the baskets costs, even down to the 6 pieces of 2 inch tape that secured the shipping box, but how much do you mark everything up? I wanted to be fair but I had to make a profit.

After speaking to several people, I was still confused. Most said that in a retail environment a mark up may be 40 - 50%. Others said the wholesale cost should be multiplied 2 or 3 times.

My wholesale Rep gave me a formula that someone gave her: If a customer wants a $100 basket, take the first $25 and set it aside for yourself. Take the remaining $75 and divide by 2, or $37.50. This $37.50 is the total wholesale cost of the items you will use to create the basket. Simply put, this is equivalent to multiplying the wholesale cost of your products by 2.67.

With so many formulas I was totally lost. I would calculate a price on a basket and then wonder - "would I pay $65 for this?" Some of the time my answer was "no" ... so now what?

Let me give you a few more things to think about and then I will give you my answer.

During the month you spend X amount of time creating new baskets, taking photos, cropping and adjusting the photos, creating descriptions and updating your website.

Your web hosting fee is $XX per month.

You go to the post office a couple of times a week. Your time is valuable and gas is not cheap. Depending on the size, a PO Box is about $60 per year and this adds about $5 per month to your expenses.

Your merchant account might charge a statement fee of $10 and an additional minimum of $10. So even with no sales this month you are paying at least $20 for the privilege of taking credit cards. Add to that the sales fee which can be an additional 4 - 5%.

Do you have a free business checking account? I hope you have shopped around but most banks charge for commercial accounts. Some charge per item, even for deposits! Add a statement fee and perhaps you pay $20 per month for the privilege of having a commercial account.

You purchase packaged food so you don't have to worry about health inspections, etc., but what if you leave a product on the shelf too long? You can't take a chance of making someone sick, so you throw out the questionable items and lose that revenue.

If you don't discard the questionable items and someone gets sick, you are the first one they will look to for reimbursement of medical bills and lost wages. You must have insurance and a simple liability policy may be about $350 a year. This is an added $30 per month.

I am not going to detail all of the extra costs here, but I want you to realize the "behind the scenes" costs of doing business. Your customers want the best deal they can find but if you don't price your baskets with these other "invisible" costs in mind, at the end of the month everyone gets paid except you! Price for profit from the start and don't feel guilty about it.

Remember that you are offering your customers a valuable service. With a single telephone call they turn their shopping over to you. They don't have to take time out of their busy schedules to go shopping, come home and wrap their gifts, package the gift for shipping and then stand in line at the post office. Saving your customers time is a valuable service! Look at it this way when you are considering the price of the basket....it is more than just products!

\* \* \* \* \* \*

Determine the wholesale cost of everything in your basket, including the basket.

For example:

| | |
|---|---|
| 7 inch Texas Basket | 3.15 |
| 8 ounce Frosted Pecans | 3.50 |
| Spicy Steak Rub | 3.00 |
| Trivia book | <u>5.95</u> |

$15.60 (wholesale product cost)

## Methods for determining your markup:

1) Multiply your determined wholesale cost by 2.5.

$15.60 X 2.5 = $39.00 retail

2) Multiply your wholesale cost by 2.67.

$15.60 X 2.67 = $41.65 retail.

3) Another way is to multiply the wholesale cost of the products in the basket by 2 and then add your actual packaging costs.

$15.60 X 2= $31.20 + 5.00 for wrap and packaging = $36.20 retail.

Now you have three suggested retail prices to consider. This sounds terribly complicated but it really isn't. Sometimes I would take all of my calculations, add them up and divide by the number of totals that I had added.     $39.00 + 41.65 + 36.20 = 116.85 / 3 = $38.95.

Taking all of this in consideration, the basket falls in the upper $30 range. All of your figures are close which is cost verification using more than one method. In this case I might sell the basket for $39.95 or even $41.95, after rounding to the nearest .95 or .99 cent increment.

Use these calculation methods to get you started. Once you price your baskets a few times, you will find a simple, yet profitable, formula that works for you.

\* \* \* \* \* \*

When your supplies arrive you will know exactly what everything costs and you can complete the following exercise. Set a timer when you begin and write everything down as you go through each step.

1) Create the largest basket that will be on your website as if you were making it up for a customer. List everything, starting with the container, all of the products in the basket, even the label you put on the basket's underside, the two business cards you put in the basket and even the number of glue dots it took to secure the items.

2) How many handfuls of shred did it take to fill your basket? What is the total number of handfuls in the box? You will need to know this in order to calculate your cost.

3) Finish it up by measuring the amount of shrink wrap film you pull off the roll to enclose the finished basket. Be sure to note the width of the shrink wrap as well as the length.

4) Add another label to your list for the front of the basket, add a bow and a gold card and about 6 inches of clear tape to secure the bow.

5) Double wrap the basket in 1/2 inch bubble wrap and place it in an appropriately sized box with 2 inch spacing all around according to UPS specifications. How many feet of bubble wrap did it take? The cost would be the cost of the roll divided by the total feet in that roll times how much you used.

6) You should use at least 3 straps of 2 inch wide shipping tape on the bottom of the box, and five if it is a heavy basket. Measure the length of one of the strips of tape and multiply by the number used. Calculate the cost of the total length used.

7) The bubble wrapped basket should be in the box on top of two extra layers of bubble. Stuff around the basket with clean, crumpled, unprinted newsprint paper in all corners to keep the basket from moving. The cost of the newsprint would be the package cost divided by the number of sheets in the package times the sheets used.

Lay more bubble wrap on top to completely cover the gift.

Keep track of how many one foot wide sections of bubble wrap you use as well as how many sheets of newsprint.

8) Holding the box securely closed, give it a shake from side to side and gently turn it over, checking for any movement of the basket in the box. Add more bubble or newsprint if necessary. Hold the box closed again and check for movement, repacking until you are satisfied that the basket will not move in the box. Add any additional bubble wrap or newsprint used to your sheet.

9) Close the box and tape it shut using at least three, preferably five strips of 2 inch tape. Measure these and add them to your calculation sheet.

10) Before shipping you would need to generate a UPS label and receipt which will use ink and 2 sheets of paper, unless you have rented a printer from UPS in which case they furnish the supplies.

11) Finally, take all of this information, calculate each individual cost using your suppliers' invoices and add it up. This is your true wholesale cost. By creating your largest basket you have determined the most that the wrap and box could cost for any size basket you offer.

Leave nothing out when you are doing your calculations. If you add a brochure, add the cost. If you add an advertising specialty, add the cost. The dollar amount of labels, gift card and business cards inside the basket will remain the same, no matter the size of the basket.

You will arrive at a cost per basket for everything else that it takes to complete an order, in addition to the gift basket and it's products. Our cost ran about $5 per basket to wrap, box and complete. Local costs vary so write everything down as you go through the steps, trying not to forget anything.

You have also learned how long it takes you to complete your largest basket from start to finish. Use this as a guideline later. If you know how long it takes you to complete your largest basket, and get it ready to ship out, you will know how much time you will need to complete a rush order.

To determine any other basket's final retail cost, add the product cost, then add the wrap/box price determined in the previous exercise. The added wrap/box cost will be a little high for smaller baskets since this was the price for your largest basket, but that is ok.

<u>One final thought</u> - When you are establishing the costs of your baskets you should know the very least that you can create a basket for and still make a profit. In our case, the cheapest basket that we would do was around $40. Anything less than that may have paid for the products and the overhead but left no profit. Without the profit you won't be able to stay in business very long.

At the end of the book are several forms and information sheets you can use to make it easier when figuring basket costs and custom orders.

**A Pricing Story:** As I said before, pricing my baskets was something that I found difficult. Over time I learned that what seemed expensive to me, was not to someone else. This is especially true in different parts of the country and with corporate clients vs individuals. Let me tell you the story of our signature basket, the Texas Giant.

When I first started the company I ordered almost every size Texas shaped basket that our manufacturer made. I didn't know what sizes I would need and if you have ever looked at the shape of Texas, I didn't know what products would fit in the Panhandle and West Texas areas of the baskets.

One of the baskets that I received was a 22 inch wide monster. I set it aside since I didn't think I could sell it packed with enough products at a price someone would pay. I concentrated on the 15 and the 18 inch basket sizes instead.

One day a corporate customer called and said that they liked all of our products but wanted something special and asked if we offered a larger basket. I told them that I had a 22 inch basket not shown on the website and they said that that would be perfect. When I asked what they wanted in the basket, they said everything I had to offer. I said that I would work on the basket and call them back with a price and the shipping cost.

After playing with products for about an hour, I called them back and told them the basket would be $129.95 plus shipping of about $20. This was $50 more than my most expensive basket on the website and I really did not think they would buy it. To my surprise, they did. They didn't even bat an eye. "Great - send it out!" Wow, was I shocked.

I took several pictures of the basket before sending it out and as a joke I put it on the website naming it the Texas Giant. What I thought no one wanted because it was so expensive, turned out to be our signature basket and the one the Wall Street Journal labeled a "best value."

# Chapter 7
## Shipping

## 1. Shipping Options

One of the most important decisions that you will make is which shipping company to use for deliveries based on the services you need. Are you willing to let a package be dropped off on someone's doorstep or do you need a signature or delivery receipt?

Where are you willing to ship your baskets? Will you ship only to USA addresses or are you willing to ship overseas? Shipping overseas and to Canada requires forms listing the contents of the boxes. Some countries assess Value Added Taxes (VAT) or gift taxes on incoming packages. Shipping to USA addresses only will simplify your shipping especially during the holidays.

Military packages going overseas must be sent USPS and usually takes six to eight weeks for delivery. Also, there is no tracking or delivery confirmation for military packages once they arrive at the post or station.

Once you have an idea of where you will ship and what services you may need, call the shipping companies and ask the following:

1) I run a business out of my home, will you pick up packages at a residence? Is there an additional charge?

2) If you don't pick up at a residence, where is the closest drop off point that accepts packages? (Some drop off locations only accept flat, overnight envelopes.)

3) What paperwork is required if I ship to Canada or outside the US?

4) Will I have to pay the customs or taxes due? Do you pay these charges and then bill them later on an invoice?

5) Are there any special packaging requirements or markings on the boxes that I need to be aware of?

6) Can I insure the packages against breakage? Is there an extra cost for this service or is it included?

7) Can I get a tracking number for my packages and how often is the system updated? Is there an additional cost for this service?

8) If one of my packages is lost in transit or broken, what should I do?

9) Does your website allow me to create a shipping label? Can I calculate the cost prior to printing the label?

10) Do you guarantee delivery dates? What happens if you miss the date?

11) Can you notify me and my customers by e-mail when our packages are delivered? Is there an additional delivery confirmation cost? (This one feature will save you countless hours and worry at Christmas.)

12) How much do you charge for daily pickup?

13) How do I pay you? Do I have to pay for each shipment or do you invoice each week?

14) If I need a package rerouted, or picked up and reshipped, can you provide this service and how much do you charge?

If I have 100 packages going out in one day, can you handle this volume?

Perhaps you can think of a few more questions as you talk to the shipping company's representatives.


## United Parcel Service - UPS - www.ups.com - 800-PICKUPS (800-742-5877)

I will admit my blatant bias for UPS - United Parcel Service - I love this company!

For years they delivered for me and never gave me grief. When we first started I used their site to print a label and arrange for pickup.

We are approximately 40 miles east of the main station for UPS in the Dallas area. When I first started the business I felt the urgent need to get the baskets out the same day and save every penny I could. One day I received an order rather late in the day, got it ready and away I went to the main station. It took me an hour and a half and approximately 3 gallons of gas. I learned very quickly that the couple of dollars they charge for pickup was a real bargain, saving me both valuable time and money!

Search their website for UPS Stores and drop off stations in your area. Be sure the location will take packages and is not just a drop off box for overnight letters. Call the drop off location and ask "if the labels are on the boxes, is there a charge to drop off a package?" Since some of the locations are owned by individuals, they may charge a drop off fee.

When we first started I arranged for a daily pickup starting the first week in December and ending the last week of the year just for the Christmas season. This daily pickup service now costs between $11.00 and $22.00 per week, depending on how much money you spend with them in that particular week. I never paid more than the minimum pickup fee during in this 4 - 5 week period. This daily pick up service will assure you that UPS will come everyday about the same time and you can concentrate on your baskets and your customers. When you start out a daily pickup may not be necessary but is very beneficial during the Christmas season.

You will build a friendship with your UPS driver once he finds out about your business. One year when we were extremely busy, our driver came two times a day. Remember, we are out in the country and our driver had a very long delivery route. He would come early and drop off the multitudes of supplies that I had ordered and around 6 or 7 he would come back when his truck was empty so he would have plenty of room for our packages. He could do this because it did not take him out of his way on the delivery route or on his return trip. This was unusual and as our area has grown, UPS has added trucks that only deliver and others designated only for pickups, so it is very possible you will have two drivers during the holiday period. If you get extremely busy and find that you are needing the supplies early in the day but want your packages picked up later, talk to your driver or the supervisor at their distribution center. They will do everything they can to accommodate you if it does not interfere with getting their packages back to the hub in time to meet their own deadlines.

United States Postal Service - USPS - www.usps.com - 800-ASK-USPS (800-275-8777)

The post office has convenient locations to everyone. If one office is too busy, there is usually another just down the street and around the corner. The US Post Office has improved their service with updated equipment and tracking methods. I have found that they are higher in price than some of the other carriers when you add tracking, insurance and notification services that are included with the other carriers. The tracking system is not updated very frequently and you may not be able to track your packages quite as well as you would like.

The US post office is the only carrier that will deliver to a PO box. I generally would refuse to send a gift to a PO Box unless we had no other option. There is no assurance that the package will be delivered by the date your customer wants them to get it. Some people with PO boxes only pick up their mail once a week and they may miss getting their package on their birthday, etc.

You must use USPS for packages going to a military addresses - APO or FPO, but some of the other carriers will deliver to a military base if the recipient has a US street address. The packages will go to the gate and then they will be notified to pick them up. There is additional paperwork to be filled out for military packages also. Pick up several forms to keep in your office and fill them out prior to taking them to the Post Office to save you time. You will have to list everything in the box and it is much easier when you are looking at the basket instead of trying to remember its contents standing in line at the Post Office.

In all fairness, the USPS has a free service to pick up packages at your door, but you must notify them in advance. If you only have a couple of boxes going out and you like their service, this may work for you. If you want to use USPS, go to your local post office and introduce yourself to the Postmaster. Let them know about your business and ask what they would suggest to make their life and your business run smoother. Also be sure they can handle the enormous amount of packages you could be sending during the holidays.


Fedex and Fedex Ground - www.fedex.com - 800-GOFEDEX (800-463-3339)

Check in your area but in the past Fedex would not pick up packages at a residential address. The policy may have changed or be different in your area. In our area Fedex delivers but will not pick up.

Fedex Ground is a separate operation from Fedex and some are operated by individuals who purchase a franchised route area.

Independent Delivery

If you need local delivery or same day service, check into an independent delivery service that will pick up and deliver. These services are generally expensive and the fees are calculated on mileage and with minimum set fees.

Ask how long it would take after you call until pickup and when you can expect delivery. Can they get a signature on delivery and is there an additional fee for this service? Are they insured for theft and liability? Ask for a rate sheet, per mile rate, etc.

You can find services in your local area using the yellow pages. Call around and keep the information on file for future reference.

<u>Local Florist</u>

If the deliveries are local, talk to one of the area florists about delivering for you. If your deliveries can be worked into their route, it is more advertising for them. Also, the amount you pay reduces their costs if they are delivering in the same area. They may not want to take on the added liability and responsibility or they may welcome the added income. It never hurts to ask.

<u>Using Your Own Vehicle</u>

I don't recommend this option for several reasons:

1) Making deliveries yourself takes you away from the office, missing calls and losing production time.

2) Using your personal vehicle for deliveries will label it as a business asset, subject to increased commercial insurance premiums and restrictions. Generally a personal auto policy will not pay for a loss if it is discovered the vehicle was being used for a commercial delivery. Check with your insurance agent. When your business grows, the purchase of a company vehicle with commercial insurance may be right for you.

3) In some states, the counties levy an annual tax on business inventory and assets, which would include your personal vehicle if used in the business.

My recommendation would be to use UPS, USPS, Fed Ex or a delivery service for all of your supplies coming in and all of your gifts going out.

# 2. Packing For Safety

The way the shipping companies throw, drop, pitch and shake your boxes is truly unkind so expect this treatment and pack accordingly!

If you are in doubt as to what you need, visit your local shipping supplier and take several different sizes of baskets with you. They can show you what they carry or can order to fit your needs. Ask to see different types of boxes, bubble, clean newsprint, peanuts, other types of filler and shipping tape. Ask for their suggestions.

Bubble Wrap - Use 1/2 inch heavy weight bubble wrap for baskets with lots of glass. For our baskets I would purchase the larger 48 inch, 250 foot rolls, perfed every 12 inches. The perfs let you cleanly rip off as much as needed. I would buy two rolls at a time - one cut into two rolls, each 24 inches wide, and the other one cut into three rolls, each 16 inch wide. The 16 inch width was perfect for the smaller baskets and the larger 24 inch width worked for our larger 22 inch baskets.

Having these big rolls cut to your specifications shouldn't cost you any extra. A roll of 250 feet, perfed at 1 foot, costs about $65, or .26 per foot. In contrast, an office supply will usually carry only the small bubble wrap costing $10 for 5 foot, or $2 per foot which is not cost effective.

Some of the larger supply companies, such as ULINE, carry heavy weight bubble wrap and can deliver very quickly, but charge over $125 a roll plus shipping.

Tape - When choosing your shipping tape, don't scrimp. The cheaper light weight tape is worthless. It will wad up and frustrate you when sealing your packages. You don't have to buy the extremely heavy tape, just a good medium tape. The lightweight tape is cheaper but the aggravation is just not worth it.

Boxes - To determine the box sizes that you will need, measure the exterior of your baskets, allowing an extra 2 inches on each side and 2 inches above and 2 inches below your basket filled with products. Usually you will purchase your boxes in straps of 15 - 25 boxes each.

# 3. What To Charge For Shipping

When establishing your shipping costs, you have a couple of options.

If your website is set up to connect to UPS, FedEx or USPS you can ship for their calculated costs. You can also set up your account to add a small fee in addition to their shipping charges.

Another way is to establish a shipping chart based on the cost of your baskets. This is the method we used in charging shipping fees. A cost method chart may look like this:

| | |
|---|---|
| Up to $40.00 - | $10.95 |
| $40.01 - $75.00 - | $12.95 |
| $75.01 - $100.00 - | $15.95 |
| $100.00 - $175.00 - | $18.95 |

The actual fees listed above should not be used - this is an example only - establish your own chart according to the current rate being charged by your particular shipping company.

Since shipping fees are charged on the size and weight of your packages, use the online calculators for the services that you might use. Determine a zip code that is farthest from your location and then input the weight and size of your boxes. By using the farthest zip code, this should be the most that you could be charged for that particular size basket.

You will start to see a pattern for your baskets. Perhaps baskets in the $50 range weigh about 5 pounds and the $75 range weigh about 10 pounds, for example.

We are in North Texas so I would calculate our charges using a New York and a Washington state zip code. I knew that our smallest package weighed 5 pounds and our largest weighed 23 pounds and I also knew the box sizes for these gifts. This gave me a starting point and the top fee for our shipping charges.

In your original research you should have made notes on shipping fees that other companies were charging. Review those notes and compare them to the fees you are considering and make any changes that you think necessary. You may want to add a couple of dollars to each of these figures to allow for fuel costs, etc.

Keep an eye on these costs as you send out your baskets to see if what you are charging covers your actual costs. There is a place on the custom order form to put what you actually paid in shipping and what you charged the customer. You can also make a note on the website orders as to what you actually paid for that particular package.

As we would ship, we found that on one package we would make a couple of dollars profit but on the next we may have lost a little. At the end of the month compare what you collected to what you actually paid out for delivery costs. This will be your guide to know when to adjust your shipping fees.

If you need to adjust your fees, don't forget to update your Terms and Conditions pages on the website and any other page you have these shipping figures listed. If you note the individual shipping charges on each basket's product page, go in and adjust these also.

If a customer orders several baskets they may expect you to send out all of the baskets for a single fee. Be sure to note on your shipping fee schedule that these charges apply to each basket shipped. You may want to extend a special shipping price to a customer who purchases multiple baskets.

# Chapter 8
# Your Website

Your website is your most important national marketing tool. It should tell your customers about your products and fulfilling your customers needs. Express how you are different and what you will do to earn their trust and their business.

## 1. Choosing An E-Commerce Host

One of the most critical things to the success of your business is the selection of your website host. This will be a company responsible for making your website available at all times, 24/7 for your customers. You are literally trusting them with your store, so take your time and ask questions. You will be interested in a shared business web hosting account. A dedicated server is not necessary until your company becomes extremely large.

Here are questions you need answered:

1) Are they the actual hosting company or are they a re-seller? Sometimes you can't tell and sometimes they won't to tell you. A cheap price usually indicates a re-seller but not always. Try to deal only with an actual hosting company. They will be your first line of defense if there is a problem. If a problem arises with a re-seller, after you contact them they have to contact the host taking longer to get a problem resolved. A reseller isn't going to be aware of a system problem but a true hosting company would actually monitor the system and servers 24/7.

2) Is there at least a 30 day money back guarantee if you are not satisfied with the service?

3) Will they give you a performance guarantee? A good company will guarantee a 99% uptime or they will refund part, or all, of your monthly hosting fee.

4) Do they offer unlimited toll free telephone technical help?

5) Is their technical help limited to e-mail assistance only? (This is fine if it is not a pressing question, if your website is down this is unacceptable.)

6) Do they regularly back up their systems and make copies of your website and all e-mails on their server? (If the server crashes this will keep you from having to re-create your site from scratch. Always keep a copy of your website yourself in a safe place. Your hosting company can direct you on how to do this.)

7) Do they have redundant power backup? Is there an onsite power generator or power back up system in case of lost power?

8) Are their facilities physically secure with fire protection?

9) Is their data center temperature controlled? (Servers are extremely sensitive to the heat and cold.)

10) When you call, do they speak to you in a language that you can understand or do they expect you to be a computer geek?

11) Is their customer service handled in-house?

12) Do they have virus software running on your e-mail and hacker protection on your website server?

13) Are they PCI compliant? If you accept credit cards on your website this is critical. You may not know what PCI is, but they should and they should know if they are compliant. If they don't know what you are talking about, go to the next company on the list, this is too important to leave to chance.

PCI is short for Payment Card Industry. Data Security Standard deals with your payment security online. Read more on the subject at www.pcicomplianceguide.org.

14) Do they offer Secure Socket Layer (SSL) encryption? Is it free or an added expense? SSL Security is encryption for sensitive customer information on your shopping cart and checkout information. This function needs to be turned on when you have your site up and running and your host can help you do this. So how do you know if it is active? When you are in the checkout area, look at the browser address. Your address should now be https://yourwebsite.com - indicating that it is secure. Also, there should be a tiny lock either at the top or the bottom of the browser page and it should look like it is closed and not open. If you do not see either, or both of these, contact your host immediately.

15) Ask about their server's download speed. They are going to tell you that the speed will vary by website and the number of photos on your site. You can control some things that may slow your download speed, but not the server. If the company is running old servers or has too many sites hosted on your assigned server, your site's download speed will suffer. Internet customers are patient to a point but a slow website will lose visitors and customers.

16) How much disk space will you need? If you have a home page, about us page, terms and conditions, contact us page and a shopping cart, you are not going to need a lot of disk space. Don't pay for space you won't use. The control panel will give you statistics on how much you used during your busiest time. Try a smaller package when you start and "step up" if you need to later. Some hosts will let you "step down" to a different package. This is fine if it offers the same features but not as much wasted space. Don't feel bad about asking because this frees up space that they can sell to a new client. Ask about fees since some companies will charge you to increase your package but will not refund any money to decrease your hosting services.

17) Website Builder - Is one provided and is it easy to use? Is there an additional cost for the website builder?

18) Do they provide tutorials or video instructions on how set up your website, e-mail accounts and shopping cart?

19) Is there a Control Panel for all of the features that come with the hosting package?

20) Do the websites have automatic e-mail responders? An automatic e-mail can be set to send to your clients when they place an order or when you are out of the office. A responder should also be set to send a copy of any orders you get to your personal e-mail. If one server is running slow, having two notifications is an assurance that you won't miss anything important like a new order. Warning: Since you will be getting two e-mails with the same order, check your order numbers carefully so you don't fill an order twice!

21) Which shopping cart software do they offer?  Are there any restrictions on the number of products in your store?  Most hosts will furnish more than one option for you to use.  Some hosts charge for a license to use the software, others do not.

Shopping carts like OS Commerce, Agora, Cube Cart and Zen Cart are usually free but most hosts do not offer any help and you have to figure them out on your own.  Others like Miva Merchant usually come with a higher cost for hosting or a licensing fee but the host will offer assistance and help.  Find out if there is any assistance in setting up your shopping cart before you sign up.

Ask your future host for website addresses that are using the shopping carts they offer.  Do you like the way they look and the way they navigate? Go through the ordering process and pick the one easiest to navigate for your customers.  You can always improve the look but not the way it operates.  If a customer's shopping experience is too complicated, or confusing, most will just leave.

How many pages or steps are required to check out?  The fewer the better.  Try to find one that has a one page checkout process.  The shipping charges, taxes and other fees should be on the first page.  If these charges are on the last page, and not what the customer is expecting, they will abandon the cart and the purchase.

If a customer has to leave before completing a purchase, does the shopping cart save their items for later?

Does the shopping cart have a "wish list" so the customer can save an item for later purchase?

Does the shopping cart allow a promo code?  You may want to run a special only for your customers or newsletter readers.  Giving them a promo code to be used at checkout is a treat for customers.

Does the shopping cart require a customer to register in order to make a purchase?  Try to use one that does not require registration.  Some customers only want to make a purchase and leave.  If they are required to register you may lose the sale.

22) Will the hosting company support the software they offer?  You may think this is a joke but it isn't.  At one time I was attempting to switch to another hosting company offering Miva Merchant which I was familiar with and loved.  This company said it would not be a problem switching hosts, but their techs did not understand Miva or could help me make it work.  After three weeks of constant frustrating telephone calls and e-mails, I exercised their 30 day money back guarantee but lost a $99 setup fee.

23) Do they offer certifications through Trust-Guard or McAfee Secure?  What is the cost?  These services offer certified PCI scanning of your website on a daily basis and they validate its security.  Customers tend to shop more at stores where they know that their information is secure.

24) How many e-mail accounts do they furnish with your account?  You will only need a couple of e-mail addresses to start.  For example:  info@yourwebsite.com, order@yourwebsite.com, customerservice@yourwebsite.com, ups@yourwebsite.com and perhaps a personal one for e-mails sent directly to you.

25) Do they offer domain name pointing and what is the fee?  Domain name pointing allows you to purchase other versions of your domain names to keep them safe, for example: www.yourwebsite.com, .net, .biz, etc. This keeps others from acquiring similar names and misdirecting your customers.  Instead of having a website for each name, the names are pointed to

your main .com name.  When someone puts in one of the other names they are automatically re-directed to your website.  Domains can be purchased from any seller and pointed to your main site.  Even if you don't have the extra domains pointed to your website, consider purchasing them just to protect your "internet real estate" and your good name.

26) Are there any set up fees?

27) Is the first year domain name registration free?  What about the years after the first?

28) How much is domain name privacy?  This is a service that lists the registrar in the WHOIS.com (www.whois.com) registry instead of your name and home address.  This cuts out a lot of spam, unwanted mail and possible website theft.

29) Does the hosting fee include a dedicated IP Address?  If not, how much is it?  The IP address is an online address that won't change, expressed in a series of numbers instead of an alphabetical domain name.  This is necessary with any e-commerce business.

The next list of features would be nice:

1) Does the shopping cart provide UPS, Fedex or other shipping company connections to a shipping calculator and online support?  You may want to use a graduated shipping fee chart but if you don't, these calculators are great.

2) Does the website come with any type of analysis or statistics? Is there a charge?  This will allow you to find out how many visitors you have had, what browser they use (so you can make sure that your website looks perfect on that browser), which pages are viewed the most, etc.  Very valuable information and some analysis packages are more detailed than others.

3) Do they offer search engine submission tools?  This can help in the initial submission to the different search engines.

4) Do they offer search engine optimization (SEO) tools?

5) Is there a mailing list manager or data base of your customers?

6) Is there a chat function? This is becoming popular - an instant messaging system between you and your customers.  There may be additional charges for this feature and it only works if you are online at the same times as your customer.

7) Is there a guest book feature?  It is nice to have customers leave comments about their experiences.  Be sure you control the content and can remove any undesirable or off-color remarks.  If you can not control the content prior to it being posted on the website, do not install this feature.

\* \* \* \* \* \*

Free website hosting services are available but I caution you not to use these.  Since they can shut down at anytime without notice, they are not the dependable host you need for your business.

The following websites review and rate hosting companies.  Generally there is a separate section for e-commerce hosts.  Some of these sites receive payment in return for a favorable listing so investigate their recommendations thoroughly.

www.alreadyhosting.com - top 10 web hosting companies.

www.hostindex.com - top hosts, domain registration, e-commerce hosts.

www.hosting-review.com - top 10 with customer reviews.

www.hostreview.com - hosting search - top 10 host awards.

www.myhostingreviews.com - web hosting directory, reviews, seo tips, marketing tips.

www.reviews.cnet.com/web-hosting/ - trusted site with forums and reviews.

www.tophosts.com - search for best host for your blog.

www.top20websitehosting.com - shop by price or by review.

www.webhosting.resourceindex.com - find a host - articles about hosting.

www.webhostingsearch.com - hosting search, wordpress, e-commerce.

## Leaving your hosting company.

Let's say you have been with your hosting company for years and have established your e-commerce presence. When do you know you need a new hosting company?

1) Your website seems to be down more than it should be - which should be never. Jayde - www.jayde.com - offers a free service that sends you an e-mail when your site goes down and another letting you know it is back up and how long your site was down. Send this report to your hosting company for a refund if they have an uptime guarantee. If this happens often, or they won't honor their guarantee, you know it is time to find another host.

2) Your customers complain they can not get from one spot to another on your site. Their computer sits there waiting for the server. Hopefully you will realize this problems before your customers start calling.

3) When you call your hosting company to report a problem and they say that everything is functioning properly. Yeah, right!

4) When you call with a question and find out they don't know how the software they offer works.

When you decide to leave, have your website complete with the new company before changing the DNS (domain name system) to point to the new host. Once it has been transferred and the new site is operating correctly, only then should you cancel the old web service.

# 2. Creating Your Website

Your business is unique and your home page is your "front door" to all of your wonderful products! Most web hosting companies offer templates to use for your new website and this will be the quickest and easiest way to get your site up and running. These site building tools are as easy to use as a word processor, with the ability to move things around and drop them where you want them. The host will usually be able to help with general questions and any problems you may have.

When you visited your competitor's websites you found things that you liked. You can incorporate these items into your website, but do not copy their site. Copyright laws apply to websites. If you like the fact that their links are at the top of the page and their basket pictures are on the front page, by all means emulate these items.

Make your site unique by adding a section that can't be found on any other site. For example, we had a section of Texas Trivia that everyone loved. We also listed the holidays or occasions for that particular month at the very top of the home page. On the first of each month we updated these sections. Since you are specializing in regional gift baskets, add a section about your state or tell about something that happened in a particular month in history.

Software: If you don't want to use the website builder furnished by your hosting company, there are website development software packages that you can purchase. Frontpage for Windows is a powerful product but may be too heavy weight for your first website. Before you choose to use Frontpage, ask your host if they support this program because some do not.

A great product for the MAC is RapidWeaver (www.realmacsoftware.com/rapidweaver). Very simple and easy to use with lots of theme and layout choices.

Some word processing programs will enable you to create a simple website and then save your work as a web file or in HTML format.

Another option is to use something like iWeb for the Mac. A program that will let you create a webpage layout. You can then use a free FTP program, like Cute (www.cuteftp.com) or FireFTP (www.fireftp.net) to upload the webpage to your hosting account. Add hyperlinks to connect to your shopping cart where your products, descriptions and prices are added. Create other pages for Contact Us, About Us, Terms and Conditions and Ordering and Shipping Information with hyperlinks joining these pages with your home page and shopping cart.

No matter which way you choose, once your home page is uploaded and running, view it using different browsers and using both an Apple MAC computer as well as a Windows PC. You will find differences in the look of your site when viewing it using browsers like Safari, Firefox, Internet Explorer or Chrome. It will also appear differently using the same browser but viewing your site on a Mac and then on a PC - same browser, different operating system. This can be very frustrating. So what are you to do?

First of all, use fonts that are recognized by all computers - Arial, Courier, Times Roman, etc. When you use fonts only recognized on one system, the other systems have to compensate by picking a font it thinks is close. Don't let your customer's computer pick how your webpage looks! To add interest to these somewhat plain fonts, you can use bold, italic or underlining and change the text colors. Remember that simple is best and don't get carried away. Play with the fonts until you are satisfied with the way your home page looks.  Using bold text on your webpage lets the search engines know the text is important.  Use bold text to emphasize keywords throughout your home page.

Photos:  You need lots of great photographs on your website but you must reduce their size or they can cause your website to slow down.  There may be unwanted items in the background that you need to remove or crop out of view.  Most digital cameras come with computer programs to manipulate the photos and reduce their sizes.

Preview on the MAC can be used to open a photo, adjust its size and then save it.  Google's Picasa (www.picasa.google.com) is free and has both MAC and PC versions.  If you display a group of pictures on a page, have all of your photos the same height so there will be some consistency.  Save your changes using the JPEG or JPG extension.

Once you add photos to the website, include alternative text (ALT Tags) for your images - a description of the picture in words.  This wording will show even if someone has their images turned off in their browser. These descriptions or phrases are included when the search engines are exploring, so this is one more place to use important keywords.  The photo descriptions should be brief, just a line or two, and must describe the image or product.  Put no more than two keywords in the photo descriptions.  Your website creator will allow you to easily add this Alt Text.  Make it a habit to describe each of your photos when you add new ones to your site.

There are programs that will let you secure your pictures so they can not be copied or stolen from your website.  While this shouldn't be a big concern, if you are worried about someone stealing your photographs, or your website content, you might consider a free service from Copyscape (www.copyscape.com).  Their service will let you search the web for information that may belong to you on other websites.  They also have a fee based service that is more automated and will check the internet automatically.  I have never had a problem with people using my pictures but if yours appear on another website, e-mail them and politely request they remove it.  If they don't remove the picture, a second e-mail suggesting copyright infringement should do the trick.

Shopping Cart:  Develop your shopping cart with pictures, detailed descriptions and prices of each of your baskets.  Each page of the shopping cart will give you a "link location."  Use these "link locations" to create hyperlinks using your basket pictures.  When a customer clicks on a basket photo on the home page it will take them directly to the shopping cart and that particular basket's detail page.

All of the shopping cart pages should have the company name, address, telephone and e-mail contact information on the top.  Most important, have a 'Home' link right under this heading so they can find their way back to the main page of your site.

Things NOT To Do:  When you are designing your website, NEVER - NEVER - NEVER do the following three things which will get you banned from the search engines.  These techniques are called stuffing or spamming, and are quite dishonest.  If you ever hire someone to optimize your site and they use one of these techniques, get a new service.

1) Never put items that do not have anything to do with your business on your site, for example, "Aliens land in Dallas." Some websites use current events and public people to attract the search engines when their site has nothing to do with those subjects.

2) Never put a "list" of key words on your site. Have you ever visited a site and at the bottom is a list of every big city in the USA or every product they have or don't have?

3) Never use the same color text as your background. Some websites will list or stuff hundreds of keywords on their site using this method. Visitors never see this because it becomes invisible but the search engines pick it up and when caught will ban you.

Finally: Check all links on your website. Do they take you where they should? Broken links are an aggravation and if your customers can't get from one place to another, you lose sales. Check all links in a browser prior to uploading a new or changed home page or website.

Siteliner (www.siteliner.com) will let you explore your site for free once every 30 days. This service by Copyscape will find broken internal links on your website and even give you the size of your website. Much easier than clicking on every link on your site!

At least once a month send a test order through your website to be sure your shopping cart is working properly. Be sure to mark the invoice as a void or test for your bookkeeper.

Spell check and grammar check your website. Proofread everything before uploading. Let someone else read the copy. Sometimes they can see something you can't or find something that may be difficult for them to understand. A second set of eyes really help.

Once complete, put a copyright notice at the bottom of the page with a date, for example: "© D. Miller 2013. No part of this website may be copied without prior written approval."

When you have been in business for a while, it can be really fun to see what your site looked like two years ago or even how a competitor's website has evolved over time. Use the Wayback Machine (www.archive.org) to see what a website looked like in the past. This site does not always include all of the photos but it is really fun to see the progression of a site over time.

# 3. Photography

A good digital camera is a must for your website photos but you don't need to buy the best that is available. Your photos should be scaled down to fit on the website. This reduction will enable your website to load quickly. The quicker your site loads, the happier your customers will be.

Use a draping cloth to cover a table for the background. This should be a solid color that shows off your basket. A white cloth may be too washed out against a natural basket. Try a royal blue or a burgundy. Take a few shots and see if you like the results. Digital pictures are easy to erase if you don't like the look. Once you decide on a color, use the same cloth for all of your basket photos to give your website a uniform look.

Arrange the items in the basket using your basket combinations. Make sure all of the products are visible in the basket.

It is best to place lights above and on the sides of the basket. There shouldn't be any shadows visible. Get as close as you can or use the zoom function on the camera. I found it easier to step away from the basket and use the zoom function rather than my macro setting.

When you work with your photos, crop or cut out everything but the basket. Make all of the photos the same height. If there are several photos together on a page, being the same height will look much better.

Give each photo a descriptive name. The name should not have any spaces and save it using either a .jpeg or .jpg extension - for example: texasbreakfast.jpeg.

# 4. Content Pages You Need

## (a) About Us

A great place to put information about you and your new company. Do you have an interesting story on how you got into the business? Tell it in a way your customers will know you are passionate about the business. End the page with why they should do business with you and make them believe it. Include where you are located and tell them you are looking forward to helping them with their gift selections.

If the company is just you, don't say, " I run the business at night with the help of my puppy in a spare bedroom after I come home from a full time job." That isn't going to win a corporate customer's confidence! You want to assure them you can do a good job and deliver on time. Never lie or be deceptive, but sometimes it is best not to tell everything. When we were recognized as one of the USA's top 5 regional basket companies by the Wall Street Journal, what they did not know was that the company was just me - a company of one!

<u>Example About Us:</u>

*Our company began in 2002 when our founder tried to locate a Texas coffee mug for a gift. Almost everything she found was made in China. As she continued to look, she noticed that gift basket companies were selling items not actually made in Texas but were calling their products "Texas Gift Baskets." The company was born to fill the need of an insulted Texan!*

*We promise to:*
*1) Only sell items Made in Texas. Our baskets are even Made in Texas!*
*2) Sell only quality products in substantial sizes.*
*3) Create a basket worthy of the title "Texas Gift Basket."*
*4) Always put our customers first! We love what we do and we love our customers!*

*Our baskets have gone to the White House and to the Texas Capital! We have participated in the Commissioning of the USS Texas and we have gotten rave reviews from the WSJ. Isn't it time that you experienced our great products and service?*

*Please help us spread a little bit of Texas throughout this wonderful country of ours! The next time you need to send something really special, send an authentic Texas Gift Basket from XYZ Baskets of Texas!*

**(b) Contact Us**

List everything the customers needs to know in order to contact you:

Company Name
Owners Name - optional and sometimes preferable to leave out.
PO Box Address - NEVER put your home address on the website.
City, State, Zip
Telephone Number - NEVER your home telephone number
E-mail address - such as info@yourbasketcompany.com - If your website has a contact form, use a link to the form instead of listing your e-mail address to reduce spam.
Business Hours - Mon - Fri and Sat, if different. Include your time zone since internet businesses are open 24/7.

Example Contact Information:

*Business Hours: Monday - Friday 8:00 AM - 6:00 PM Central Time*
*Saturday 9:00 AM - 3:00 PM Central Time*
*E-mail: customerservice@yourgiftbasketbusiness.com*
*Mail: Your Gift Basket Business, PO Box 222, Your Town, State, Zip*
*Phone: (555) 555-5555*

**(c) Privacy Policy**

Customers want to know what you are going to do with their information. If they know you will protect their information they will have more confidence in your business. In this day of unwanted e-mails and sales calls, and with the new laws concerning solicitation, assure them in writing that their information will only be used to contact them about their order or specials you might be running.

A mailing list is a very valuable asset of any company. Never sell your list and only use it for your own promotions and state that in your privacy policy. If you use your list for e-mail marketing, always include an easy way for customers to opt out. If a customer requests their e-mail to be taken off your list, do it immediately.

Example Privacy Policy:

*We send out e-mails to individuals who would like to know about our specials and new products. You may remove your name from our list at any time. We do not share or sell our customer list or any customer information to anyone!*

**(d) Order And Shipping Information / Terms And Conditions**

This information should be available to the customer before they place an order with you.

Product Guarantee - Assure your customers that their satisfaction is your ultimate goal and you will make them happy.  You may state a specific guarantee or a more general one.

Example Product Guarantee:

*Our Texas products are gourmet quality and we are sure that they will meet or exceed your expectations.  Please contact us if you every have a question about one of our products.  Our main goal is the satisfaction of our customers.*

Shipping Rates and Shipping Issues - Always state your shipping rates, whether you use a rate chart or if it is based on the amount of their order.

A note about using a graduated shipping scale:  Be sure to indicate that the prices listed are for each basket to be shipped.  At Christmas, some of our customers would expect us to ship all of their packages for a single shipping fee even though they were going to separate addresses.  If a customer purchases multiple baskets, you may want to adjust the shipping charges and give them a discount.

Be sure to include any additional shipping type incidentals. A good example is a $10.00 address change fee that UPS imposes if the package has to be re-routed because of the wrong address.  UPS will bill you for the change and you can pass it on to the customer if you make them aware ahead of time.  Impress on them to be sure the address they are giving you is correct and includes any apartment or suite number as well as the street address.

If your shipping rates do not include expedited shipping, such as overnight or 2nd day air, state your policy on this type of package.  Will you bill them the actual cost?  Let them know the regular shipping charges do not include these expedited services.  Some customers will actually expect overnight or expedited services for the ground rates you state - that is when you refer them to this section.  Calculate the actual fee for these services and make it a policy to contact them for approval prior to charging their credit card and shipping.

Also, be sure to state that if a package is delivered to the address that you were originally given, and it has to be picked up and re-delivered, the additional cost of the re-delivery will be charged to the customer.  If the mistake is yours, admit it, don't make excuses, apologize and pay the additional shipping yourself - it is going to happen.

It is very important to contact the customer about any additional costs.  Note on your copy of the invoice who you spoke with, the time and the amount that was approved.  I have had customers request overnight service that quickly changed their minds when they were told the shipping cost was as much as the basket itself!  Suddenly, ground service at our normal rates would be fine.

Do you only use UPS?  Do you only deliver to street addresses in the USA?  On deliveries to Hawaii and Alaska, does your shipping rates still apply or will you calculate the actual cost and contact them? Put that information in this section.

103

<u>Example Shipping and Delivery:</u>

*We ship via UPS Ground to the Continental USA to street addresses only, Monday through Friday. We try to send your orders out on the same day we receive them or the following business day, if placed on a weekend or holiday. Please allow 4 - 5 business days for delivery.*

*Military packages ship via USPS at our actual cost. Packages going to Hawaii and Alaska will be billed at cost and we will contact you prior to shipping for your approval. We do not ship outside the USA so please allow additional time if you need to forward your gift to another location.*

*Address changes are $10.00 per package after we have shipped your package unless it was our error, in which case there will be no additional charge.*

*Please note: If your basket is going to a hotel, the package must be called for at the desk. Hotels will not deliver a package to a room, they will only hold them for their guests to pickup. If a hotel delivery must be picked up and redelivered by UPS, you will be charged the actual cost of the pickup and second shipment.*

*If you need a package to arrive by a certain date, please let us know. If necessary we can ship our packages Next Day Air, 2 Day Air or schedule a Saturday Delivery but these services are charged at our cost and not at our standard Ground Shipping Rates. We will get your approval prior to using these methods and let you know the charges prior to shipping.*

*Our Standard UPS Ground Charges are as follows:*

*Up to $40.00 -          $10.95*
*$40.01 - $75.00 -      $12.95*
*$75.01 - $100.00 -    $15.95*
*$100.00 - $175.00 - $18.95*

*If your package arrives damaged, contact us immediately. Keep all of the original packaging and broken products. Put the damaged basket back in the box, tape it closed and get it ready for UPS to pick up. We will issue a pickup ticket for the damaged basket that should arrive at the same time as your replacement basket.*

<u>Payment options</u> - What credit cards do you take? Do you take orders over the phone and through the mail? Do you take checks? Any special payment arrangements?

<u>Example Payment Options:</u>

*We take American Express, MasterCard and Visa credit cards for payment. We do not take checks or CODs. Purchase orders are not accepted and we do not invoice.*
*Large orders are charged 1/2 down and the remaining 1/2 plus delivery fees when the order is shipped. <u>This policy does not apply to holiday pre-orders</u>. Please contact us prior to placing a large order to verify that we can supply your needs in a time frame that will be to your satisfaction.*

Product substitutions - At some point you <u>will</u> run out of an item and while you are waiting for replacements someone will want a basket that includes that item. What do you do? Always put in a similar item, or two, that is at least the cost of the item that you are out of and state this policy here. Let your customers know that you will make every effort to always have the items on the website but occasionally substitutions will have to be made. Make a note on your copy of the invoice, what you were out of and what you substituted, for future reference if the customer should call.

<u>Example Product Substitution Disclaimer:</u>

*We try very hard to always have our products on hand but occasionally our suppliers can not meet our needs. We reserve the right to substitute similar products of equal or greater value in our baskets if necessary.*

*If you would like to make a substitution or an addition to one of our baskets, just let us know by e-mail or phone. We love doing custom baskets, so just ask!*

<u>Holiday Order Information and Schedule</u> - Let your customers know just how busy you will be during the holidays and ask them to order early. This will allow you to order enough supplies early. Nothing is more disappointing to you and your customer than to tell them "no" at Christmas! You should also stress that at this busy time package delivery will take longer than normal - another reason to order early.

<u>Example Christmas and Holiday Orders:</u>

*Happy Holidays! The Holiday Season is our busiest time, so please place your orders early! Send us your orders now and your credit card will not be charged until the order ships! Place Your Holiday Orders Now!*

*1) Order online - just indicate a December delivery date or*

*2) Large orders, or multiple address orders, please call or send us an e-mail or fax with your gift list. Let us know which baskets you want, and where they are to go, and we will do the rest!*

*Normally our packages arrive in 4 - 5 days, but during the holidays please allow more time for your gifts to get to their destination. We offer expedited delivery services at additional cost if you need these services.*

<u>*We Will Stop Taking Orders On December 15th, So Please Order Early!*</u>

## (e) Question And Answer Page

A question and answer forum might be nice and something that the other basket companies are not doing. Think of things that your customers might like to know about until you start getting real customer's questions. Once you start getting questions, update this area often.

The Q&A might go something like this:

***Does your products contain MSG?***  No, none of our products contain MSG.

***If I send a basket to someone, do they have to know who sent it?***  No, just let us know that you want to send it secretly and we will mark the order accordingly.

***Are your baskets made in Texas or China?***  Our baskets are handmade in the Red River area of Texas, never from China!

### (f) Blog

A great area for short announcements, giveaways, contest or to keep your customers up to date on the coming holidays.  You can highlight a particular basket for the month and tie it in with a holiday, such as a Grilling Basket for Father's Day or a Chocolate Basket for Valentine's Day.

This would also be a great area for giving out recipes that use the products you carry.  Most of the manufacturers that you will work with will have recipes to highlight their products.  Just ask them for permission to include these on your website and be sure to give them due credit for the recipes.  The more your customers know, the more they will want to use your products.

## 5. Monitor Your Website

You have put a lot of work into your site and once it is uploaded it will be running on auto pilot, so how will you know if there is a problem?  You can't check the site every few minutes and you need to know as soon as possible if the site has a problem.  Go to InternetSeer (www.internetseer.com) and sign up for their free website monitoring service.  They will check your site everyday, record the speed of your website and send you an e-mail report once a week.  This service will also alert you by e-mail when your site is not responding and another e-mail telling you how long it was down.  This is a great service for free.  They also have other, more detailed paid services that you may want to explore.

Nothing is more aggravating than a slow website and it will cause your customers to leave prematurely.  Check the speed of your website by going to www.webpagetest.org.  If your site is slow to load, first check the size of your photographs.  Reduce the pixel sizes if needed.  If this is not the problem, contact your hosting company for assistance.  They may have you on an older server or one that is overloaded slowing yours down.

## 6. Website Optimization For Better Rankings

Companies can pay a premium to appear on the first page of a search engine's results.  A page resulting from a search contains two separate sections - paid sponsors and the top 10 of hundreds or more sites that the search engine determines is pertinent to the search requested.

The search engines use algorithms, closely guarded, always changing, secret formulas that will either shoot your site to the top of a search or put it where it will never be seen. The search engines continuously "crawl the web" looking for just that right combination on every site. If you get on the first page of a Google search, you are probably in the top 10 of the other major engine searches as well - Bing, AOL, Yahoo, Excite, etc. One way to succeed is to let Google help fine tune your site:

Google Webmaster Tools - www.google.com/support/webmasters - Webmaster tools, articles on website optimization, free services and testing your site.

Google Analysis - www.google.com/analytics - See who and where your visitors are coming from and where they go once they are on your website. Find out what your customers are looking at or ignoring.

Google + - www.google.com/services - Google business solutions.
　　　　Also check out:

Internet Marketing Ninjas - www.internetmarketingninjas.com - great SEO tools as well as webmaster tools such as spell check, screen resolution, keyword density and more.

Site Pro News - www.sitepronews.com - lots of articles about how to improve your website and search engine rankings. Free webmaster tools with lots of referrals and resources for different aspects of your business.

Seochat - www.seochat.com - provides some great forums to read and tools for almost everything you need to optimize your site.

SeoWorkers - www.seoworkers.com/tools/analyzer.html - site analyzer and a spell checker for your website.

Three very important things that you need to address in creating your website:

1) Title tag - very important! This is what will appear in the browser bar. If a visitor bookmarks your site, this is what they see. Your main keyword, phrase, or product should be first in the title followed by your company name.
　　　　For example - Texas Gift Baskets by Miller Gift Baskets.
　　　　Title tags should be about 60 characters and spaces.

2). Meta tag or description - This is a short complete phrase that identifies you and what you do. This is the phrase that the search engines pick up on and is the description you use when registering with the search engines. I have seen a phrase that I used 5 years earlier still coming up in the description of our site even though I changed the meta tag several times over the years. Think about your meta tag description because it could be with you for a long while!

For example: Wonderful food and gifts from the great state of Kansas - great for those away from home or just arriving. Kansas Baskets uses authentic Kansas made products in a Kansas shaped basket - also made in Kansas! Proud members of the Kansas Department of Agriculture's "Go Kansas Program."

The meta description should be in full, descriptive sentences and are usually from 50 to 150 characters and spaces. Google only displays the first 154 characters of any description.

3) <u>Keyword tag</u> - There is a controversy as to the importance of keywords. These are words or phrases that someone would use to search for your regional gift baskets. Use one or two words separated by commas that directly relate to your site, your product or item list or your location. Do not repeat a word more than two times.

For example: Texas Gift Baskets, Corporate Gift Baskets, Salsa, beans, chili, hot sauce, gourmet food, Dallas Texas, Texas Gifts.

Keywords should be limited to 4 - 8 words or phrases and approximately 250 characters and spaces.

If you need keyword suggestions or alternate ideas, check out the free service Ubersuggest (www.ubersuggest.org). Input a keyword and it gives you multiple suggestions.

Only use the title, meta and keyword tags one time in your HTML code, per page. Some sites think they will get a better rating if they duplicate these tags several times on the same page but duplicates are seen as spam.

# 7. Submitting To Search Engines

The search engines continually "crawl" the web looking for sites to fill their customers requests. In the past it would have taken several weeks "to be found" but now it can be only a matter of hours.

How do you know if you have been "found"? Use Google or Bing and search for your company name in quotations. Your site will come up if you have been indexed by that particular search engine. Check the description that the engine gives your site. Notice the cached date - this is when their crawler last visited your site. Make a note of this date and check back in a week or so and you should see another cached date. Now you know about how often that engine tends to crawl your site. If you have new information for your website, go ahead and change it without trying to time the search engine crawler. What the search engines do, how they do it and when, changes all the time!

When I started my company in 2002, MSN would guarantee that your site would be crawled on a regular basis for $30 per year. I grabbed this chance to get noticed. At that time it could take months before a search engine would include your site. MSN was the largest search engine at the time and this service made a world of difference. I did not make a single sale on the internet the first several months but two weeks after MSN "found me" I started to receive orders from all over the USA. The orders came in on a consistent basis after that and then along came Google.

Our site was always ranked about # 5 - #12 on MSN and we did fairly well, but when our site went to #1 on Google in March of 2007, our business doubled and in some months, tripled. We stayed #1 until I sold the business.

Search engine ranking will not only make a difference in your monthly income but in your overall company's worth when it is time to sell.

You can submit your site to the search engines and directories or there are services that will do it for you. Check with your hosting company because most include a submission service as part of their hosting fee.

At the bottom of most search engines is a link to "submit a site." If you would like to submit to the search engines one by one, it will take only a day or so. There are only a handful of the largest search engines that everyone uses.

What about the hundreds of other search engines? There are services that offer to submit your website to 300+ search engines for a fee. In my opinion this is money better spent on products. Most of these smaller search engines no one has ever heard of or used. If you submit your site to the larger 4 or 5 search engines and some of the directories, the rest will find your site.

Here are a couple to get you started:

www.Bing.com/toolbox/submit-site-url - Yahoo is included in the Bing engine.

www.dmoz.org/add.html - Web directory that several of the larger search engines (AOL, Google, Netscape, etc.) use to locate websites. Make this your first submission but be careful to submit using the correct category.

www.entireweb.com/free_submission/

www.google.com/submityourcontent/website-owner/

www.jayde.com/submit-site.html - Submit your site for free - Jayde B2B Search engine. Free webmaster tools on the site.

www.manta.com/website_submission - Business directory - list for free.

www.scrubtheweb.com/addurl.html - Add a listing for free - website tools, information to improve your site and a meta tag analyzer.

www.submitexpress.com/free-submission.html

www.submitterbot.com - free submission to 500 search engines and directories.

Wonder where you are ranked on different search engines? Check your pagerank for free using Internet Marketing Ninjas (www.internetmarketingninjas.com/tools/) or PR Tracking (www.prtracking.com).

# 8. Buying Search Engine Placement

The top section of a search results page is a listing of paid sponsors. By purchasing keywords for a fee the company is given a premier spot when someone searches for that word. There are a couple of opinions on companies that pay for those positions:

1) The company is perceived to be a larger company that offers better products and better service. How else could they afford to purchase this highlighted spot?

2) Other people won't even look at these companies. Quite often they do not have the products that you are looking for and have purchased keywords and ad placement to get you to their site. Why? Because that particular key word is popular and while they may not carry the product, they hope that you will find something else while visiting their site.

3) Some people feel companies that have "bought their rank" don't deserve their time. They trust the search engines' ranking that the unpaid sites actually contain what they are looking for.

Use your own judgement in determining whether the purchasing of keywords would be a benefit to you. I would advise against it, especially in the beginning. Did you know that each time someone clicks on a sponsored link, a fee is due and the majority of individuals visiting are "just looking?" Something else to consider, if your competition wanted to hurt your advertising efforts, they could spend all day clicking on your sponsored site listing, wasting valuable advertising dollars.

# 9. To Link Or Not To Link

A link to your site means a better ranking on the search engines. If one hundred legitimate companies put links on their site to your site, be thankful. An exception to this is 'link farm' or sites that sell you a listing on their site. Listings on this type of site can actually hurt your rankings.

What about sites that will list your site if you reciprocate and list their site? You have no control over who they list, which could be your competitors or something morally inappropriate.

I made the decision not to link to anyone. I listed associations that we were part of, and other companies that we did business with, but never a clickable direct link. I did not want our customers going anywhere other than links within our site. Once a customer clicks outside of your website, you have a chance of losing them.

Links are also distracting. Have you ever gone to a site where there are so many links that you forget why you went there in the first place? Or worse, you click on a link, go outside the site and then you can't find your way back to the original site? Unless it pertains to something you are offering, I would suggest not including outside links in your website.

Additional income is the reason for most outside links. Companies like Amazon, Google and countless others offer payments to websites to include their advertising. When you sign up, you will be given a couple of lines of code to include on your website. When a visitor to your site clicks on one of these links, you get paid a fee. The added income may be attractive but why divert your customers from your site? Provide excellent regional gift baskets and superior customer service and highlight yourself.

If you are curious about who is linking to your site, check out the Backlink Checker (https://ahrefs.com/index.php). This service is free but they only allow three queries per day.

# 10. Guest Books

Guest books are usually part of the hosting package that you can turn on or off. As long as you have full control over the guest book, you may want to consider this option. Nothing is better than praise from your customers: "Great service, quick and efficient, great product selection, great customer service" - who wouldn't want that on the front page of the website?

What if a customer (or competitor or personal enemy) posted a negative comment and you did not check the website for a couple of days? Absolute disaster! If you can edit <u>any and all comments</u> on the guest book prior to being published, use this feature. <u>If you can't, don't.</u>

# Chapter 9

# Promotion And Marketing

How do you get customers?  How do you keep the customers you have?  How do you know what your customers want?  Here are a few ideas:

## 1. Business Cards

The best advertising that you can have, after your website of course, is your business card. Purchase a nice set of cards with thermography (raised ink) or foil if you can afford them.  These are your representatives when you are not there, make them speak of quality.  Use classy colors and don't get silly with too many logos and several different types of fonts.  Simple, yet elegant.  Let the card speak for you - this is who I am and this is my specialty.

Be professional and hand these out at every function you attend and every chance you get!

When ordering your business cards, consider a plastic or plastic coated version.  The more expensive cards tend to last longer and customers hang on to the nicer cards - they actually feel bad about throwing them away!

You may want to consider magnetic business cards in addition to your regular cards.  These are great when kept on the filing cabinet and it makes it easy to find your number when your customers need a gift!

## 2. Postcards

The best advertising method we used was a 4 X 6 inch postcard printed with a full color photograph of our largest Texas basket on one side.  The basket was filled with products but without the wrap so the products were very visible.  In the center of the basket was a small white see through cloud that had our company name, phone number, and website address.  On the back of the card was our mailing address, a list of our products and occasions to give our baskets.

These were inexpensive to mail, small enough to keep and really impressive to look at with the full color photo.  Four color postcards can be ordered locally or try Modern Postcard (www.modernpostcard.com), PS Print (www.psprint.com), Vistaprint (www.vistaprint.com) or Postcards.com (www.postcards.com).  These companies can also help you with full color magnets, stickers, labels and stamps if you don't have a local printer.

If you send out postcards each month to a different group (attorneys in January, realtors in February, doctors in March, etc.), you will soon learn which group will be your customers and which to drop from your promotional efforts.  This doesn't mean stop all efforts to a certain group but you will find certain businesses to be more receptive to what you have to offer.  Once you find those businesses, advertise to this group more aggressively.

# 3. Newsletters And E-mail Marketing

Newsletters, special offers for upcoming holidays, a coupon promotion or contest announcements can be delivered using e-mail and your customer data base. Immediate delivery and no postage costs make this option extremely attractive.

A monthly or quarterly contest drawing for one of your newsletter readers is a promotion that will encourage visitors to sign up and to tell their friends. You will have another opportunity to promote anything new, etc., when you announce the winner of the gift basket. The promise of a prize is a great incentive to get people to visit and share your website information with family and friends.

Make it easy for your customers to sign up for your newsletters and promotions. The sidebar area of your website would be a good spot to add an "opt in box" for your newsletters on every page.

You can handle e-mail promotions yourself or check out one of the following services:
Constant Contact - www.constantcontact.com - 866-876-8464. Newsletters, promotions, event invitations, e-mail marketing and online surveys.
AWeber Communications - www.aweber.com - 877-AWEBER-1.

No matter which way you decide to go, always provide a way to opt out of future e-mails. It is the law that this option be included in every e-mail that you send out. If a customer wants to discontinue receiving future e-mails, take them off the list immediately.

For detailed information on your responsibilities as an e-mail advertiser, read the FTC's CAN-SPAM Act: A Compliance Guide for Business (http://www.business.ftc.gov/documents/bus61-can-spam-act-compliance-guide-business).

# 4. Your Data Bases

Your customer data base should include name, address, phone number and e-mail address. Additional information such as which basket was purchased, an invoice reference number and the name of their recipient should also be kept. Keep two separate lists, one of your customers and another of recipients.

Duplicate your customer data base and record who they bought for, what occasion, such as a birthday and which basket they purchased. Record the date, the recipient and the occasion. Sort this data base by the occasion date and e-mail your customer a week or two before the event. Remind them of what they bought last year and suggest something else this year. Ask them to contact you if they would like to order a basket or a gift.

Your customer list is a very valuable asset to be used to request new business. The recipient list is just as valuable because if they liked their gift, they will be very eager to send one of your baskets to their friends and family.

You generally think of a customer list as a marketing tool, but it is much more. Data bases are helpful when a customer calls and wants to order the same basket as last month but wants a different message on their card. Using the data base as a reference, you can quickly go to the invoice file and pull their last order. This makes it simple to find the order and call them with the requested information.

For several years in a row I had a customer who would send an anonymous custom basket to a friend out of state. Each year they would call and ask, "What was in the basket last year and what message did I write?" A data base can make this process almost painless instead of going through all of your orders from last year!

# 5. Satisfaction Cards

Customer service should be of the utmost importance when you are creating your baskets and speaking to your customers. A happy customer will order from you again when they need a gift. The recipient of one of your baskets will become a customer if they get a memorable basket. What about all the rest? You may never hear from the majority of your customers and recipients. Wouldn't you like to know if they are happy and if you met their expectations? How do you know if you are delivering what they expect?

A stamped, self addressed postcard should be included in the box, or in the basket itself, asking for a review. If the questions only take a few minutes, and you provide the stamp, you should get almost a 100% response. Printed inexpensively these postcards could provide a gold mine of information. There may not be room on the postcard for everything, but list those things most important to you. Good customer service starts with listening to your customers, so don't forget to leave room for their comments!

Here are a few questions to get you started:

1) What was your favorite product and why?
2) What was your least favorite product and why?
3) Were the products in sizes that you could use? Too small or too large?
4) Were the products as good as they looked?
5) Did the basket arrive safely and on time?
6) Was anything broken or damaged?
7) Was the box in good shape or was it damaged?
8) Was the box opened before it arrived?
9) How was the condition of the gift itself?
10) Was the product presentation impressive?
11) Would you recommend our gift baskets to your friends and family?
12) Will you order from us in the future?
13) Are there any comments that you would like to make?

Add a line or two at the bottom for comments. Ask if they would like you to contact them to discuss anything that they may have found to be unsatisfactory. This may seem like asking for bad news, but if something was wrong, this extra effort to fix the problem will be appreciated.

Most people won't complain if they get an unsatisfactory gift. They just won't buy from you or recommend your company or service. This extra effort lets your customers know you care about them. When you run an internet business, your customers and gift basket recipients don't know if you are a mom working from home or a Fortune 500 company unless you decide to tell them. Think how important they will feel when your company took the time to ask their opinion or perhaps followed up with a personal phone call!

# 6. Thank You Card And Discount

Send your customers a follow up card to say, "thank you" for their business with an imprinted magnet or letter opener.

When business is slower during the summer months, offer your customers a discount on their next order. Put an expiration date on the discount offer so they will hurry and order.

# 7. Christmas Promotional Letter

A promotional holiday letter to prospective customers should be sent several months prior to Christmas, prompting them to place their orders early. Send these letters in September or October, before someone else gets the company's holiday budget!

Tell them about your products and what makes your company special. Never put the competition down, just express the numerous ways you are better.

This advance letter will allow companies to think about their holiday buying early, make plans and then get on with their business. That is when you get to worry about their Christmas gifts!

The office supply should have blank holiday letterhead and matching envelopes that are perfect for this type of letter. This is also a great item to buy after Christmas at 1/2 price so next year you won't have to wait for the office supply to get them in.

The following is an example of a holiday sales letter with some suggestions to help you make the letter your own. Change the wording to customize it for you:

**Your State Gift Baskets**

**PO Box xx, City, State Zip**                                                    **555-555-5555**
**E-mail: info@yourwebsite.com**                                   **www.yourwebsite.com**

*(When sending to a large company, send the letter to the boss and another to their assistant. The assistant is usually instrumental in buying gifts for the company. A letter should also go to the head of purchasing, human relations and the meeting planner, if the company has these departments. The company's receptionist can tell you if they have these departments and who is in charge.)*

**Dear Mr or Ms. Customer,**

*(Let them know right away what you have to offer and suggest they buy it from you.)*

**What could be more appreciated this Holiday Season than a gift of gourmet food and goodies from Texas? This Holiday Season send an authentic Texas Gift Basket from Texas Gift Baskets.**

*(Tell them how you are different or what you specialize in and any associations that emphasize your company and products.)*

**Only items actually "Made in Texas" go into our baskets and even our baskets are "Made in Texas." We are proud members of the Texas Department of Agriculture's "Go Texan" program supporting our state's products and farmers.**

*(Emphasize the differences in your company and your products. Tempt them with all of the great products and make them want to visit your website.)*

**Our products are also substantial in size - 'sample sizes' are not allowed in our gift baskets! We have chili and enchilada soup mixes that feed 6 - 8 people. Our salsas and dips come in 16 oz jars. Our fruit cobblers are ready to eat in 17 oz jars. You will find larger sizes in our other wonderful products such as our jelly with pecan pieces, flavored pecan halves and teacakes. We carry cornbread mix grown and ground right on the farm, barbeque sauces, hot pepper sauce, grilling and dipping sauces, meat rubs, seasonings and marinades. Excellent products for those on your gift list to enjoy.**

*(Have you been recognized by any organizations, newspapers or have made appearances on any of the local TV shows? Let them know about any awards your company may have received. This a great time to toot your own horn!)*

**On (insert date) we were blessed with a wonderful review by the XYZ Journal and were voted best regional gift basket company in the Southwest. We were honored by their praise of our products and our people.**

*(Let them know that you will be very busy during the holidays and ask for the advance order - this will help you tremendously in ordering supplies for the Holidays. Give them an incentive - order now and we won't charge the card until December or 10% off all orders placed before November 1st.)*

**Help us plan for our busiest time of the year and order early in October or November. Your credit card won't be charged until your gifts are ready to ship in December. We accept American Express, Visa & MasterCard.**

*(Let them know how you ship and how long it takes. During Christmas there are always those who wait until the last minute and the fact that you can provide expedited services if necessary may get you the order.)*

We ship via UPS ground to the continental USA.  Delivery takes 5 business days or less, however, during the holidays UPS does not guarantee ground delivery times, so please order early!  Expedited services are available, if necessary, at increased cost.

*(Thank them for their time and let them know that gift baskets are great any time of the year and to keep you in mind in the future.)*

**This year we hope you will choose your Holiday gifts with us online at**

**www.yourgiftbasketcompany.com**

**Thank you and we hope to hear from you soon.  If you have already made arrangements for this Holiday Season, please keep us in mind next year.  Texas Gift Baskets are appropriate throughout the year for any occasion.  Whatever the season, or the reason, an authentic Texas Gift Basket is always appreciated!**

*(Finish the letter with your signature phrase in the foot note section of the letter.)  Something like:*

**"If it isn't made in Texas, it isn't in our baskets!"**

\* \* \* \* \* \*

Once you are satisfied with the wording, print it on regular paper.  Put this printed page behind a page of your holiday letterhead and hold it up to the light.  By doing this you can see where you need to adjust your margins and spacing without wasting your holiday letterhead.  Continue to make adjustments and reprint the letter until you are satisfied with the way it looks and fits on the holiday paper.  Once satisfied, print your letters using the holiday stationery and adding the appropriate names, titles and addresses.

Use your data base of past customers, and their recipients, to send similar letters asking for their business again this year.  Thank them for their past business, tell them you look forward to helping them again this year and wish them a Merry Christmas.

# 8. Advertising Specialties

I love advertising specialty items.  Anything that you can imagine can be imprinted with your name, information and your logo.  You can go a little crazy with cool advertising items for your company, but unless it is something that is going to stay on someone's desk every day, I would resist.

Letter openers, a large paperclip or paperweight, magnets for the file cabinet or break room or a desk type calendar large enough for notes are all good choices. Pocket calendars and calendar holiday cards are usually discarded on January 2nd.

How about a paperweight with your business card imbedded in Lucite?  A little pricey but good for your best customers.  Tell them they won't have to dig for your number!

For a larger office consider an imprinted candy jar for the receptionist's desk. Everyone will see your name and you can occasionally send candies to refill the jar so it is certain to remain on the front desk.

Pens are great until they run out of ink. The exception would be a Quill or a Cross that are just too good to throw away. You might want to get a couple of these for your very best customers and then occasionally provide them with a refill and a reminder that your business is always thinking of them - it will make an impression.

You can use advertising specialty items in your actual design. Canvas bags with your company logo and website printed on them can be filled with goodies and wrapped with a plume. New plastic paint buckets with your information can be used for Father's Day and filled with goodies. When the goodies are gone the bag or bucket remain with your company name and website always in front of them!

Advertising specialties are all around us so look for ideas that you can use in your designs. Thomas Registry (www.thomasnet.com) can be used to locate actual manufacturers in your state but call and ask if they actually produce the items. Many of the manufacturers are only warehousing items made overseas. Always think local and verify.

# 9. Donations

Donating a gift basket can be great advertising for your business. One of my favorite events was the annual Chamber of Commerce fund raising auction. The baskets were displayed and put up for auction and our business cards were made available for everyone at the event.

One of the most exciting things that our company was involved in was the Commissioning of the USS Texas in 2006. The Commissioning Committee contacted us about donating a basket for the event. We always favored military requests and this one was special! The ship was the USS Texas! To add to the excitement was the list of dignitaries participating in the ceremony - First Lady Laura Bush, the ship's Captain, our two Senators, the Governor and a past President and First Lady!

Did we want to send a basket to the First Lady? I didn't think twice! They only requested one basket but I sent six of our biggest for each of the special guests. Wow, what an honor to request our baskets! The committee wanted an authentic Texas gift basket and ours were just what they were looking for! When the baskets arrived they were so thrilled they honored us with special tickets to attend the Commissioning and treated us like royalty! This was a special honor and totally unexpected! The Commissioning brochure even listed us as one of the sponsors of the event!

As you grow, you will be contacted about donating to all types of causes - worthy and not. Decide early who you will contribute to because the requests will come pouring in. Choose a couple of charities that are dear to your heart and stick to those. If you give to everyone that asks, you will be giving away more merchandise than you can sell! I was always polite and explained that I had certain charities that I supported and just couldn't add any more to my list at that time. The e-mail requests and letters were easier to handle.

Evaluate each request on its own merit but remember you have more right to say "no" than they do to ask. Don't let anyone make you feel bad if you say "NO."

Another form of donation that I should mention is companies wanting a 'free sample' prior to ordering. Often they will tell you that they will be placing a very large order and want to be sure of your products. Offer them a sample basket at your cost plus shipping. If they are not willing to pay for the basket, even at a discounted rate, I would suggest not sending them anything. The few times that I did send 'free samples,' the companies never purchased anything and I lost my products and the shipping. Reputable companies do not mind paying for what they receive.

# 10. Personal Promotion

You may be lucky enough to be located close to downtown or to a concentrated business area. If you are in an area close to a business park or multi high rise buildings, you have a distinct advantage over your country cousins. A ready made advertising opportunity!

Take a day off and visit these buildings, going from floor to floor. Take notes on who is in the building and which floor. Go home and call the largest company and ask for the senior administrative assistant's name. Once you have this, make up a basket of goodies just for her. Be sure to showcase what you do and make it special.

Go back the next day with the basket and armed with plenty of business cards, postcards and any other information about your company. With the basket in hand, stop at every office on the way and explain that you are on the way to deliver it to Ms. So & So at ABC Company and wanted to stop and drop off information for them, should they need your services. Plan to spend some time in the different offices because you will get some very curious people "ooing and ahhing" at your gift basket. This is one time that drawing attention to yourself is a good thing!

Finally, go to the intended company and ask directions to Ms. So & So's office because you would like to deliver it yourself. Be sure to walk slowly holding the basket for all to see on the way. You will get noticed and probably have some followers to the office! Once there, present the gift telling her that you just wanted to introduce yourself and the company. Let her know if she should need your services to contact you personally. Make the visit brief, leave your contact information and be sure to say "thank you" for her valuable time.

This one gift that may cost $30 in products, probably will net more goodwill, and definitely more exposure, than you could get mailing out flyers!

# 11. Bulk Mail Permit

A bulk mail permit can be a two edged sword. It saves money on large mail outs but some people will immediately find a trash can when they see the bulk mail stamp. You need them to open and read what you are sending.

If you are mailing photo postcards with all your information visible, consider using bulk mail. If you are sending out a more costly letter, like your holiday sales letter concealed in an envelope, you should use regular stamps.

## 12. Mining The Newspapers

The daily business section is full of information on businesses in your area and their chief officers. Most large companies publicly announce who has been promoted. Send one of your business cards or a post card to that individual - he may want to say thank you to his boss!

Your local Chamber of Commerce know which companies are moving into the area or who is building a new facility. These large moves are also covered in the business section of the daily paper. The main company executives are usually listed along with their titles.

The Dallas newspaper publishes a list of the largest 200 companies in Dallas once a year and another issue covers the largest companies all over Texas. Check with a large city paper in your area to see if they put out a similar issue and when. You may be able to purchase a past copy from the paper itself or find one at the local library in the archives if you know the publication date. This issue is a gold mine, full of addresses, names and titles, company website and e-mail addresses just waiting for you to advertise your baskets.

## 13. Chamber Of Commerce

One of the best ways to get to know other business people in the community is to join the Chamber of Commerce. Check with your local group to find out all of the benefits of membership.

Our local Chamber has an after hours business card swap sponsored by a different member company every month. They also hold a ribbon cutting ceremony for new members advertised in the local newspaper. The Chamber's main function is to promote your company to other members and to those moving into the area that may need your services. If you are concentrating on local customers, consider the Chamber of Commerce as a top priority.

Not only does the Chamber know who is moving to town but they help set up events and conventions that may need your gift baskets for their attendees. A close relationship to the Chamber will give you many networking opportunities outside of your immediate area.

Offer the Chamber a discount on gift baskets for their new members to be presented at their ribbon cutting ceremony. One more opportunity to market your baskets.

If you want to market to the Chamber members, their roster should be online or drop by their office for a current list.

## 14. Event Planners

Event planners are a special group of individuals that specialize in organizing events - anything from a wedding to a convention for thousands of people. Event planners can be individuals with their own businesses or employees of large hotels and marketing firms.

Wedding planners need gifts for the wedding party and out of town guests. Large hotels need gifts for companies that keep an executive apartment for VIPs coming into town. Convention and event planners need gifts for their event and as a thank you to the companies that employ them. Hotels and Bed and Breakfasts need gifts for arriving guests, special package weekends or special occasions.

Below are a couple of associations that you may want to investigate. Market your baskets to the members or become an associate member or supplier. These associations have in house attorneys, insurance and marketing specialists that you may find beneficial to your own business. You may find suppliers through the associations that you will want to use. Several of these organizations have local chapters.

Event Planner Association - www.eventplannerassociation.com

Event Planner Consortium - www.eventplannerconsortium.com

International Special Events Society - www.ises.com

National Association of Event Planners - www.nationalassociationofeventplanners.com

The local Yellow Pages will also have listings for Event Planners, Wedding Planners, Caterers, Hotels with executive housing and convention capabilities and Convention Centers in your area.

# 15. Print Advertising

When we first started we purchased an ad in a very large Texas magazine. The cost for a three line word ad was about $100 per month with a one year commitment. We didn't receive enough orders to continue the ad the second year.

We then used a national western type magazine, which fit our products a little better. This particular one was about $50 every other month and we received more responses but still not enough to warrant the cost.

Some regional publications will give you an advertising discount if you are a member of your state's logo program, so ask if they extend this type of discount or have other discounts that you can use.

You can experiment with your regional print media and see if it increases your business in your situation. In our particular case the response rate did not warrant the expense.

# 16. School Functions / Publications

Check with the area schools to see if they print any type of directory for the parents. These directories usually have advertising spaces that can be purchased very reasonably. One year we purchased the back cover of our granddaughter's directory and it proved very successful for us.

The schools also sell things like stadium cushions to earn extra money and again these will have advertising space that you can purchase. Most of the time these small ads are inexpensive.

Not only are you getting advertising that lasts a longer than print advertising, but you are helping the local schools.

# 17. Yellow Pages / Online Directories

Consider an ad in the Yellow Pages if you are concentrating on local customers and businesses. The ads can be short and sweet or take up a full page. A line ad or business card size ad is a good start. You will be committing to a monthly advertising charge that is added to your phone bill, generally for a year. There may be a discount if you pay the cost in full when you place the ad.

An advertisement in the surrounding area phone books can expand your reach if these areas do not have a gift basket service.

If you are operating as an e-commerce business only, the internet offers business yellow page listings and online directories by various companies. Take advantage of these for a local regional gift basket business as well. Here are a few to start with:

Local.com - www.local.com
Manta - www.manta.com - list your company for free.
Super Media - www.supermedia.com/Spportal/quickbpflow.do
Super Pages - www.superpages.com/addnewlisting.php - offers basic free listings.
Yellow Book - www.yellowbook.com - offers a free internet listing and also has print advertising available.
Yellow Page City - www.yellowpagecity.com
Yext - www.yext.com - free listing
Yelp - www.yelp.com

Whether you use the printed yellow pages or the internet version, verify the service is legitimate prior to signing a contract or sending any money. There are scams in this business that will take your money and then vanish. Be especially cautious with the ones that call you and offer their services. Buyer beware.

# 18. Billboards

There it is - your name in huge letters, placed in a spot for thousands of people to see - WOW! Placed in the wrong setting, it becomes one huge expense!

We checked with a local company that handles the rental of billboards all across Texas. The company proposed a billboard that would have cost $250 to set up and $600 per month rental on an annual contract. This is a lot of money, but if hundreds of people see your name and web address day after day, they become very comfortable with you. Name recognition can make all the difference in the world. The placement of the billboard is crucial. If it is on a highway connecting one small town to another, it is not going to pull the same response as one placed on Central Expressway in Downtown Dallas. More traffic equals more sales.

The rental prices are usually negotiable. If the billboard is in a prime location, the rate probably will not be negotiable and there may be a waiting list when it does become available. Once a company stakes a claim on a prime billboard, it may be next to impossible to gain access to it.

There is one other possibility.  Contact one of the smaller companies that manage billboards in an area that you are interested in.  If there is not a sign in the area you are interested in, they can contact property owners and arrange to erect a new sign just for your company.  If the sign does not violate any property, city or county restrictions, the land owners are generally eager to lease for a billboard sign.

# 19. Gift Basket Directories

Another avenue to explore is the gift basket associations and directories.  The people visiting these sites are looking to buy gift baskets of all kinds and baskets from all 50 states can be found there.

If you are considering joining one of these associations, investigate what they expect of their members and be sure you can deliver accordingly.  If you are running a home-based operation with only UPS delivery, your company should not be listed on a site that requires same day delivery.

The fees may seem high, but this form of advertising is for national exposure with a built in audience looking for what you have to offer.  The membership fees are usually paid on an annual basis.  Ask if they offer a money back guarantee if their service doesn't meet your expectations.

Ask how many visitors they get per month and how many go to your state's section.  Do they advertise in regional or national magazines, or buy keywords on Google, etc.?  Get all costs, requirements and particulars prior to signing any contract.

If you pay by credit card, ask if they automatically renew the membership or notify you prior to charging your credit card.  Next year you may not want to continue the service, so mark your calendar a couple of weeks prior to renewal to decide.  The credit card is a great way to pay for your business expenses but companies with an automatic renewal policy should inform you prior to signing any contract.  This is especially true if there are no refunds.  The last thing you need is a renewal you did not expect and no way to get a refund.

Here are a couple to check out:

Gift Basket Network - www.giftbasketnetwork.com - 928-774-7629 -
E-mail:  shopcreativegifts@yahoo.com - a text listing with a link costs $50 per year listed under the state of your choice.  A full directory listing runs $150 per year and includes membership in Gift Retailers Connection.

Gift Basket Superstore - www.gift-basket-superstore.com - Gift basket directory.  Free listing with a link back to their site.  State Sponsor listing runs $75 per year and an Enhanced Listing runs $125 per year.

Seek Gift Baskets - www.seekgiftbaskets.com - Memberships range in price from free to $51.75 for 3 months.

<u>Gift Basket Suppliers</u> - www.giftbasketsuppliers.com - this is a unique site. You can find supply wholesalers or list your business under the Gift Retail heading for $10. They have listings for all 50 states. Great site to just browse.

<u>State Specific Malls</u> - there should be a gift mall specific to your state. An internet search with your 'state' and 'gift' should pull up either a mall or association for you to join. One example is Truly Texan (www.trulytexan.com) which showcases only merchants and craftsmen located in Texas.

Individuals looking for specialty food and gifts made exclusively in your state or region would be extremely happy to locate you on one of these state specific sites. There is usually a monthly fee for advertising and linking on these sites, most seem to be around $30 per month. Ask about their promotional activities. Some state specific malls use print media advertising and rank well on the search engines, giving you good value for your monthly membership fee.

# 20. Social Media

Social Media is a good way to get more exposure for your business but they have separate rules for business use, so read the terms and conditions carefully. If you don't know how to use these, each have "getting started" tips on their sites. Also, Lynda.com (www.lynda.com) has instructional videos on how to use these sites specifically for marketing your business.

Facebook - www.facebook.com
        Business https://www.facebook.com/business/overview

Google Plus - www.google.com/services
        www.google.com/intl/en_us/+/business/get-started.html

Linkedin - www.linkedin.com
        business and professional network   www.linkedin.com/company/linkedin-company-pages-1349/product?trk=b12_products

Pinterest - www.pinterest.com

Stumble Upon - www.stumbleupon.com

Twitter.com - www.twitter.com
        https://business.twitter.com

Install "like" and "share" buttons on your home page and your shopping cart pages for the social media you have chosen to set up. Use these sites to announce contests or give weekly tips on how to use the products you offer (recipe of the week). From each of your social media sites, link back to your website, blog or to a particular basket that you want to highlight for the month.

Social Bakers (www.socialbakers.com) offers statistics for your Facebook, Twitter, You Tube, Google Plus and Linkedin sites. Free tools and free trials of their paid services are available that will give you an insight on how you are doing on these social sites.

Compare your site to the competition's on the various social media sites with Blitz Metrics (www.blitzmetrics.com). Generate reports, analyze and monitor content across several social media sites. There is a free version and a paid version to fit your particular needs.

Finally, MarketMe (www.marketmesuite.com) finds people on the social media sites that are talking about topics related to your business. MarketMe has a free service and a Pro Plan that is about $15 per month with a 30 day free trial offer. Connecting with people looking for your products gives you a distinct marketing advantage.

# 21. Affiliate Marketing

When you are confident in your business abilities and are ready to grow, check into starting an affiliate marketing program. By offering affiliates, or partners, a commission for referring a customer that makes a purchase, this is a winning combination for both of you. Unlike "pay-per-click" advertising, affiliates only get paid when a sale is actually made. Your affiliates can be an enthusiastic sales force multiplying your internet exposure many times over.

Some web hosting companies offer affiliate marketing through your website account. This is great except you have to keep up with who is registering, approving their site, keep up with their sales and paying commissions each month. To reduce this workload, consider an Affiliate Marketing Network. There are several good ones like ShareASale (www.shareasale.com), Linkshare (www.linkshare.com), Pepper Jam Network (www.pepperjamnetwork.com) or Link Connector (www.linkconnector.com).

Check their fees, minimums and other merchant requirements prior to signing up to see if they will be a good fit for you. A commission paid only on sales, may be the boost that your company needs! Since you only pay if someone produces an actual sale, this type of advertising beats a "pay per click" hands down!

# 22. Local Connections

Florist - Form a friendship with some of the local florists. Although you might think of them as your competition, they are usually only interested in flowers but have customers that call and want something different.

Work out a business arrangement with them to market your baskets and then call you for the order. You deliver to their shop and they deliver the basket. In your agreement, state their commission rate and if you will be allowed to put your business name on the basket. They may only want their business name on the basket.

Another suggestion is to get the florist to refer customers to you in exchange for a finders fee - 10% - or whatever you agree upon. Be sure to keep a separate sheet for each florist, the date, the customer and the price of the basket so you will know how much to pay them at the end of the month. Don't pay commission on taxes or delivery, only on the basket cost.

<u>Consignment</u> - Consignment sales with local merchants is something that never worked for us.  Usually the store wants 40% of the retail price and that pretty much wipes out any profit for you.  Your products are displayed, handled and possibly abused and if damaged or stolen the store generally does not pay you - you take the loss.  If you try consignment sales, make sure the commission is in a written contract.  In that contract state that you will be paid the retail basket cost, less the commission, if the basket is broken, stolen or the store has a disaster and the stock is lost.  They probably won't agree to this but ask anyway.

<u>Display</u> - An alternative to consignment sales would be to place a basket or two of non-perishable items on display with an area merchant. If someone wants a basket the store can call you to make a fresh basket for the customer and then you pay the store a commission.  This arrangement may work out better for you both.  They get a referral fee (which should be much smaller than the 40% consignment fee), you don't take up their valuable shelf space and the customers get fresh products.

# Chapter 10

# Work Day - Making Baskets

Keep the original order with you from start to finish.

1) Pick a basket or container and check it for nicks or imperfections. Wipe it down with a soft cloth to remove any dust or those tiny glue strings that some manufacturers leave on their baskets. Also by using a soft cloth you will find any staples, nails or ends that could puncture your products, shrink wrap, you or your customer! Remove any hazards or put the basket aside to return to the vendor.

2) Put your label on the bottom of the basket or stamp it. Don't cover up the manufacturer's mark, if there is one.

Assemble your basket on a towel next to the turntable. You may find the turntable aggravating since it will spin while you add items to the basket.

3) Fill the basket with shreds if it is a flat basket. If using a deeper basket, use clean crumpled paper at the bottom topped off with shreds to cover the paper.

4) Using your basket info sheet, pull the products that you will need from the shelf and assemble them in the basket. Alternate glass with plastic or paper containers - no glass against glass. The items should fit tightly together but not crowded.

5) Once the products are in the basket and you like the arrangement, use your glue dots to secure the products to one another. On some of the larger glass items put glue dots on the sides as well as the back. This will insure that the softer items act as a buffer and the glass items will remain in place.

Some designers use glue guns but I would discourage their use. The glue is hot and can damage your product packaging, burn you and leave tacky strings on the baskets. The glue also does not provided a cushion between your products like the glue dots. The glue dots are quicker and much cleaner.

If you need more cushioning between products, and you feel shreds won't be enough, cut a small piece of thick cardboard and place it between your products. Anchor to your products on both sides with glue dots and cover the cardboard with shreds to hide.

6) Tuck a business card or other ad specialty item just under one of the front products, but don't bury it in the shreds.

7) Take a second look at the basket and its contents. Is everything cushioned and anchored to your satisfaction? Are the products placed to make a great presentation? Make any final adjustments necessary.

8) Pull out the folded shrink wrap on your machine, lift the finished basket and slide it between the wrap. You may find that you need a different size shrink wrap and need to trade rolls.

Work on the towel and the shrink wrap slides easily.

9) Seal the first seam. This will disconnect the piece covering your basket from the roll. Roll the rest back on the roll and away from the heat bar.

As you work around your basket, seal the seams close but not too close to the basket itself. When I first started I would seal the edges as close as I could to the basket and it almost always caused a seam to burst. I had to start all over wasting a lot of shrink wrap. The heat gun will shrink the wrap so leave it a little loose as you are sealing the edges.

10) Turn the basket and seal all the way around. Be careful that your towel does not get caught in the sealer which could be a fire hazard.

11) Once the seams are sealed all around, place the basket on the turntable.

12) Find a corner and cut off a tiny bit, about an 1/8 of an inch, going across the seam. This is to allow the air to escape the basket as you shrink wrap it. Do not cut a slit going into the basket because the cut will rip inward and you will have to repackage your basket. Start shrinking the basket on the opposite side from the tiny hole and work your way towards it.

13) Your heat gun should NEVER be set for the hottest setting. Set your gun at about 1/4 heat. With the movement of the gun, the dial will sometimes move. If the setting is too hot, it will burn a hole in your packaging. Make a point of checking your heat setting with each new basket.

Professional heat guns are very dangerous and should be used with extreme caution. Never let the kids play with them and never "blow" toward someone - a serious burn could occur.

Continuously move the heat gun from side to side, holding it about a foot away from the wrap as you turn the basket on the turntable. Never let it stay in one spot too long because it will quickly burn a hole in the packaging.

Shrink the top and sides of the package and then the bottom. If you are doing an upright basket with a plume, work from the bottom sides upward, doing the very bottom of the basket last. Be careful as you get close to the top gathering for the plume. Stop before you reach the plume.

14) When the shrink wrap cools, the seams can have a hard point or rough spot that can possibly injure someone. Carefully go around the basket checking the seams as you go.

If you find one of these areas, use the heat gun to go back and forth across the spot to soften the seam. If you heat it too long, the seam may burst. If this happens use a small piece of clear shipping tape to repair it. The repair is usually invisible. When the seam has cooled, but is still soft, check the spot again to be sure it is no longer a hazard. The plastic wrap gets very hot so use caution.

15) Attach your ribbon or bow, the gift card and finally your company label. If you are using a flat tray type basket with a raffia bow, the wrapping of your gift will be much quicker and will arrive looking fresh.

16) Wrap the package using enough bubble to go around the package twice and then use another strip of bubble to go around the package the other way, also twice. Now you have 2 inches of bubble on the top and bottom and at least 1 inch on the sides. Secure the bubble with tape and set the basket in a box.

Add crumpled paper on all sides and on the top. If you are using peanuts, a heavy basket will slide around unless you solidly stuff them all around. A better way would be to secure the sides of the basket with clean paper and use the peanuts only on the top of the basket.

Close the top flaps and while holding the package secure, turn it over. You should not hear or feel any shifting or rattling. If you do, open the flaps and add more packaging. If there is movement, the basket can work its way to the edge of the box and the chance of damage increases. If the packaging is not sufficient and something breaks, UPS will not reimburse you. Once you are convinced that the basket is not going to move or shift, tape the box lids down the center and on both sides of center.

With a marker put the recipients' name / senders last name and the order number in a small area on the box lid. Weigh the package. With UPS the weight is the next even pound, so 1 1/2 pounds would ship at 2 pounds, etc. Put the weight of the package just above the names on the box. These notations should be confined to a small area so they can be covered with the shipping label.

Across the top of your order form note the box size used and its weight and put the order form on your desk to charge the credit card and make a shipping label.

Your box should go to the holding area with the other boxes waiting on labels. Do not put these packages with the boxes that have labels already attached. Make labels for your boxes throughout the day. Don't wait and do them all at once because your shipping driver could come at any time.

Now you can go on to the next order.

17) When you have completed several orders, run the credit cards for your orders going out that day and note the authorization code on the order form. Always run the cards prior to making any shipping labels.

You may have a few cards declined, for whatever reason. If this happens, first verify that you input the correct card number, CVV code or zip code for that order in your Virtual Terminal or machine. If you did this correctly, call the customer and verify that you wrote the correct credit card number down right. Usually a declined card is just an error on your part or the customer reading off the wrong number. Credit card numbers are very long and this is the cause for most declined cards.

If the information you have is correct, explain to them that their card was declined and ask if they would like to use another. The customer will probably want to contact their credit card company and call you back. Put a large "HOLD" in red on the order and tape it to the box in the holding area. When they call back, they may give you another card number or ask you to attempt to charge the same card again. Usually this resolves the problem.

18) Once you have received payment, make the shipping labels. Only make labels for those packages going out on that day - do not make any labels for a future day's shipment.

Write the tracking number on the order form and the amount that you paid next to the shipping fee that the customer paid. The completed label should be matched with a box in the holding area. Cover your notations on the lid with the shipping label and move the box to today's ship out area.

During Christmas you will be completing several baskets that will be held for a future day's shipment. Always check the holding area first thing in the morning for those packages needing to go out that day. Charge the credit cards and then make labels for those particular boxes before starting any new baskets that day.

When you make the labels, there will be an area for a reference note. Use the name of the person ordering the basket and the order number for your reference. Circle this information on the label using red ink, or some other bright color, to attract attention. I have had individuals call me to say they did not order anything, or since they did not know who the box was from they were afraid to open the gift! By putting something like: "From Mary Jane Doe #1019" or "Merry Christmas from Mom & Dad #1019" and circling it in red ink, they know who it is from immediately. This also gives you an invoice number reference in case the recipient calls with a problem.

If you use UPS, take advantage of their free service called Quantum View Notify. When you make the label, input the e-mail address of the person who ordered the basket and your own e-mail. It would be a good idea to set up a separate e-mail address for receiving only these UPS notifications, something like: ups@yourbasketcompany.com. Quantum View Notify allows 5 e-mails to be sent per package and even has a notation area that you can say "thank you!"

When you input your customer's e-mail address, they immediately get an e-mail letting them know their package has been sent, they get an e-mail if it gets delayed because of weather and they get another e-mail when the package is delivered. It provides a link to the tracking system so you know where the package is at all times. The system is updated throughout the day and will let you know when it is delivered, if it was left on the doorstep or who signed for the package at the company dock.

Now you won't have to trace a package two weeks after it shipped because someone was rude and did not call to say thank you! I would recommend this service even if it incurred a fee. It saved me so much time especially at Christmas!

You may want to put an additional label on the inside of the box if it is going overseas or to an APO / FPO address. If the outside label gets damaged, customs or the post office can still get it to its destination.

19) A finishing touch for your shipping boxes would be a good quality, coated, 4 color sticker. A photo of one of your baskets in the background with your logo, company information and website address would be a classy touch and not as expensive as imprinted shipping boxes.

20) Now that the day is done, check over what you have going out the next few days and your inventory. If you need more supplies, call before the close of business or first thing the next morning. Try to stay up with what you have going out and your stock so your orders won't be delayed. Use the Purchase Order Form and make notes of anything you ordered and when you should expect delivery

21) Each day call the bank to update your balance with any deposits that may have come in. Check these against the sales you made two or three days ago, depending on what credit card is settling up with you.

In the afternoon, write down the sales for the day and any checks you wrote or charges you may have put on the company credit card. Indicate what these expenditures were for on your expense ledger. If you take time each day to update your accounting records, it is much easier to stay out of financial trouble.

# Chapter 11
## Invoices - Cart Checkout

On the final page of the checkout process, ask your customer to print out a copy of the invoice for their records. Set up an e-mail auto responder to your customer with a "thank you" note.

Make sure that all fees and charges are visible up front and there are no surprises at checkout. One area that is notorious for this is the shipping and handling fees. While you may have stated everything in your policy area, a new customer may place a quick order without reading everything.

Shipping fees: We charged shipping fees using a graduated scale, determined by the amount spent. I also listed the specific shipping charge on the page for each basket. If you have 25 different baskets you can copy and paste the statement right after the description and then fill in the amount for that particular basket. This way there are no surprises. Don't you hate it when you go to a website, place an order and then find out the shipping charges are more than the item that you just bought?! This is one reason for unhappy customers and with shipping charges going up every day, this may be the deciding factor whether they buy your basket or not.

Taxes to be collected: Don't forget about state and local sales taxes when you do your billing or input this information on the website. In Texas we do not pay taxes on food but we do pay sales taxes on items like candy and flavored pecans. If the basket goes outside the state we do not collect taxes.

Some states have taxes on items that are purchased outside the state but delivered within the state. It is impossible for you to know every rate in every state and at every level of local government.

One thing is for sure, taxes and laws are always changing. Some states are trying to impose taxes on internet purchases delivered within their state. Keep checking on this issue and what you are responsible for collecting and paying and to whom.

Custom Orders: Invoice numbers will be assigned by your shopping cart, but you will need a custom order numbering system for your phone orders. We used a date system followed by the number of the order for that date - for example: 20130501-1, 20130501-2, etc.

When you send out a custom or telephone order, mail the customer an invoice copy and a paid receipt for their credit card charge. This is not necessary on orders that come through the website, unless a customer calls and changes an order or wants to add expedited shipping. In this case print out the online order, mark any changes needed, assign a custom order number and create a new invoice. Send the customer an invoice copy and a credit card receipt.

# Chapter 12

# Handling Large Orders

One day you will get a call wanting 300 baskets and you need to think about how to handle this type of order before it happens.

Will you have enough time to complete the order if your suppliers can get you what you need? Politely ask when the customer needs the baskets completed and where they will be going so you can calculate shipping time. Can several be sent in the same box or will each one require a separate box? Get all shipping addresses and details in writing via e-mail or fax.

Which basket they are interested in or do they want something special just for their event? A customer doing hundreds, may only want a basket with one or two items along with their business cards or other business items included. If they are not sure what they want, you may need to make up a couple of sample baskets, with and without the wrapping, take pictures and e-mail to your customer for their selection.

Take all of the information down and tell them you will check with your suppliers and call them back.

Rule 1: Do not order any supplies until you have all the details completed and money in your hand.

Rule 2: Do not quote any prices or make any commitments until you have spoken to your suppliers.

Figure the inventory that you will need and call your suppliers. Can you get the amount you need and by when? If this is a large enough order, is there a discount that your supplier can extend to you? Don't forget about your shreds, shrink wrap and large boxes for the shipments.

How long will it take you to complete the baskets? Make one that is similar in size and with the items they want and time yourself. You will be doing your regular work in addition to this special custom order, so allow a little extra time. You may have to wait on items from the company to include in the basket. Most of the time they can get you their items by the time your other supplies arrive. If you need some extra help this would be a good time to see if it will be available for a day or so.

Next, check to see how long it will take for delivery from your business to the destination. Don't forget to allow for weekends, holidays or hazardous weather that could delay the shipment.

If it takes 3 business days to receive your supplies, 6 days to complete the baskets and 4 more business days to get it from you to the destination, this will tell you how much time you need. Don't forget to figure business days and to exclude weekends. Always allow yourself an extra day or so for unexpected events. If they need all 300 by Friday you know it can't be done and you should not even attempt to take the order.

Now figure your costs to complete the baskets. If you have to add another employee for a day or so, how much will this cost you? Don't forget about the packing and bubble wrap for each gift. If you need something special just for this project, perhaps a special size shrink wrap that you may never use again or larger boxes for shipping, add the whole cost to the project and not just the amount you will use.

Once you know you can get the needed supplies and how long it will take to complete the order, call the customer. Let them know you can complete their order by the deadline and the total of the order plus shipping. If they agree, send an e-mail to them outlining everything that you talked about, describe the basket in detail and the products being provided, when to expect delivery and the total cost. Check your figures a couple of times before creating the e-mail and check your figures in the e-mail before sending it to the customer. A mistype or a moved decimal point would not be good! Once you quote a price you will have to live with the quote.

On large orders, collect 1/2 of the total when you take the order and the second 1/2 plus shipping when the order is complete. Usually the initial 1/2 down is non-refundable but use your own judgement on this issue. If the company changes their mind after you order the supplies, you generally can't return the items, or if you can, it will cost you freight both ways and a restocking fee. You should not have to take a loss if they change their minds. These terms should be indicated in the original e-mail that you send. Do not order anything until you have the company's authorization for the order and their initial 1/2 payment.

Make sure that they want to use the same credit card for the second 1/2 of the order. Some companies may want to use different cards for different departments, etc. Send a receipt detailing the order and noting that the balance and shipping costs will be charged upon shipment of the baskets. Upon completion of the project, send another invoice and receipt for the total collected, showing the dates and the amounts of the two payments.

On multiple basket orders, always ask the customer to e-mail you a list of their recipients. Not only is this quicker than taking 30 names and addresses down, this provides you with a written reference with proper spelling and addresses, reducing errors.

On a large order, the shipping is generally billed at cost on the final invoice. You need to decide if you want to charge the customer the actual delivery charges or add a little extra.

Once the order is complete, send a 'thank you' gift basket so they can enjoy the same treats they purchased for everyone else.

# Chapter 13

# Customer Satisfaction

No matter how many baskets you send, eventually you will have a problem with one or more of them. Think about how you will handle this situation before it happens.

The problem may be a missed delivery date, a broken baskets, a broken product that ruined the rest of the basket or you may just have a customer that did not like what you sent. I think we replaced only six baskets for different reasons, most of which we had no control over the situation.

Only a couple of our baskets were broken and these were caused by an employee trying to save money on shipping supplies. Instead of saving money, the scrimping on less expensive packing materials lost valuable products and cost additional delivery fees. We immediately sent out new baskets and had the broken ones picked up. When these were returned I knew exactly what had happened and the employee situation was corrected.

One year two baskets went to Wisconsin during an extreme cold spell and the hot sauce in the baskets froze and exploded. Again the baskets were replaced with our apologies.

We only had one basket stolen from a doorstep which I guess is a pretty good record.

There was only one complaint in all of our years that was because of the products. A lady had received one of our baskets as a gift and she called and complained that the flavored pecans and the peanut butter candies were stale and asked that we send her more to replace the bad ones. I knew this individual was trying to get more products without paying for them because I had just received both of these products two days before I sent her basket out. The candies were handmade each week and the flavored pecans were from a new batch. I explained that the products were fresh but she kept insisting they were stale. I apologized and I told her that I would be sending her different products of equal value. She became very disappointed and kept insisting that I send the same products to her. That is when I knew for sure she really liked the candies and pecans and wanted something for nothing! I sent her replacement products but not the ones she requested.

Give a guarantee to your customers and let them know that you will do everything you can to correct a problem, should one occur. Always replace the products with items of equal or greater value than the products they had a problem with. Be generous with your customers when they have a problem and you will be rewarded with their continued support.

# Chapter 14

# Christmas Season

After a couple of years a pattern emerged that helped us estimate our Christmas volume. Whatever we did January through November, we would do twice as much in the month of December. In other words, if we sold $15,000 total baskets in the months of January through November, we would do $30,000 in December alone. Some years it was much more that twice what we did in the previous 11 months. This is not a guarantee but we found this to be true in our situation. This wasn't the case for us in 2004.

In 2004 we sold two baskets in the month of October that set the pace for our whole Christmas season that year.

A gentleman called and wanted our largest basket sent to Florida to arrive by Friday so he could present it to someone on Saturday. I told him that we could get it there and we chatted for a while and I sent the basket out. The following week we received an internet order for the same basket to go to Dun and Bradstreet in New York. Again, we got the basket out and didn't think anything else about it until November when the gentleman from Florida called again.

He asked if I remembered him and I told him I did and I asked how they liked their gift. After chatting a bit about the products in the basket, he identified himself as Charles Passy, a writer for the Wall Street Journal. He was doing an article on regional gift baskets for the holidays and wanted to include our company. The basket that was sent to Dun and Bradstreet was for pictures and to satisfy them that the separate shipments were consistent in content and in the service we provided.

The Wall Street Journal was looking for regional gift baskets that contained products actually made in that region or state. They were also checking the different company's customer service, the quality of the products, the condition of the basket when it arrived and if it arrived on time and as promised.

After chatting a bit, he told me that they did not want us to know who they were or what they were doing. They wanted us to send them a basket like we would send anyone else and not make any special efforts to impress them or their decision. The moral of the story is to make your baskets, and your service, speak for you. You never know who might order, or receive, one of your baskets!

Very early on Friday, December 3rd, 2004, I was on my way out the door when the phone started to ring. New York is 2 hours ahead of Texas time so the phone calls started very early that day. I put my purse down and I did not leave the house for the next 10 days!

The phone rang off the wall, 7 days a week and a few of my mornings started at 2:00 AM. That year instead of doubling our yearly sales in December, the figure was more like seven times. We couldn't have purchased this kind of advertising. I hope you are blessed with this kind of Christmas surprise in your business in the future!

The Wall Street Journal article can be found online at:
http://online.wsj.com/article/SB110202785325689743.html

Now it is time to prepare for your holiday season. Cool weather, glad hearts and a lot of buying going on! You will be a major part of you customers' holiday plans.

They will call you, place their orders and forget about their shopping because now it is up to you! A huge responsibility when you think about it. There are a lot of people depending on you for their holidays - not only your customers but those receiving your gift baskets.

Holidays will be different from your normal days. Usually you take an order and ship it out. During the holidays you will take orders well in advance of the shipping date and this takes more organization on your part to be prepared.

Christmas buying is usually the busiest for every merchant and hopefully will be for you. Here are my suggestions for the holiday season. This procedure also works well as your business grows:

1) First, make sure that your own holidays are taken care of for you and yours. You shouldn't be worrying about your holidays when you are trying to get out hundreds of baskets for others! Get your shopping done before Thanksgiving. This also includes getting the Christmas tree up and decorated. When you are no longer worrying about last minute plans of your own, you will be able to give your customers your undivided attention.

2) Order everything early - tell the vendors you need delivery around Nov. 15th. This gives you time to organize the supplies and make sure you haven't forgotten anything. If you wait too long, the suppliers may not be able to get your order out in time.

3) Make a file for each week of the holiday season. These folders are for the orders coming in and should be filed by the "to do" date. Within each folder, have the orders clipped together for each day of the week.

You have learned approximately how many days it takes to get a package from your location to different areas of the country. If a customer wants a basket somewhere by the 15th and it takes 4 days, you know you have to send it out by the 11th. Don't forget to check the calendar and add extra days if there is a weekend involved. Put this "to do" date on the top of the order and file it in the proper future day's file.

At Christmas you may want to add an extra day or so because of the volume of packages sent and the winter weather conditions. Usually after December 7th or so, UPS does not guarantee their ground shipping delivery dates, but in the years they delivered for me they were on time or a day early at Christmas.

4) At the start of each day, go to the file and pull the "to do" orders for that day. Check the types of baskets that will need to be done today and group them together by the basket type. In other words, if you have orders for four breakfast baskets and three sweets baskets, group those together. It is much easier to line out several of the same basket at one time in an assembly line type process.

5) As you receive the orders, make a list with columns on a pad. Put the order number, last name of the customer, which basket they ordered, date ordered, date requested to be delivered and leave a space (column) for the date that it needs to leave your office. For custom orders leave the order number out and fill it in later.

As each basket order is filled and shipped, line through it on the main list. You can quickly see if you have forgotten anything.

On a different sheet, as you receive the orders, keep a tally of the number of each type of basket. This will allow you to keep tabs on your supplies and what you need to order. Try to keep checking on orders received to be sure you have, or can get, the needed supplies in time to complete the orders you have received.

6) During the Christmas holidays you will receive larger orders than normal. On multiple basket orders, always ask the customer to e-mail or fax you a list of their recipients and their addresses. Not only is this quicker than taking 30 names and addresses down, this provides you with a written reference with proper spelling and addresses, reducing errors.

7) Set a cut off date for accepting new orders and put it on your website - preferably on the homepage. We always cut off orders around December 15th. After this we usually couldn't get more supplies in and the baskets completed and delivered by Christmas.

Customers will still call and want to place an order. If you have enough supplies to complete the orders you have committed to, take the order. Watch your shipping dates to be sure you can get it there in time.

These last minute orders may need to be sent Overnight or 2nd Day Air to reach their destination on time. If this is the case, get the expedited fee and call the customer for approval. Never send out a basket using an expedited service unless you have spoken with your customer and have their approval for the added amount. Because of the cost, they will often cancel the order or allow it to go ground shipping with the understanding that it will arrive late. If you send it expedited without their approval, they may request a refund and you should give it to them. Write on the order the person authorizing the expedited shipping, the date and time and the shipping cost.

8) By December 23rd, close down shop, put a message on voice mail that you will return calls after Christmas (some basket companies close down until Jan. 1) and enjoy your family.

9) If you open up after Christmas, try to sell the products you have in stock and don't buy anything until after the first of the year. For accounting purposes, reduce your inventory as much as possible and do not restock until January 1. Inventory in stock is not deductible on your federal taxes and some local counties will tax you on any inventory in stock on January 1st. One exception to this rule would be a supplies ordered specifically for a large custom order.

10) Most customers realize that your stock will be diminished after Christmas, but they will be needing a thank you gift, etc. prior to January 1. You may need to explain that you can't complete a certain basket that they want, but that you would be more than happy to create a custom basket just for them. These customers are usually very happy to get a custom basket instead.

11) Make a list of inventory and supplies that you need to replace, but don't call in the orders until after the first of the year.

12) Gather your records for your CPA. Complete your inventory on close of business on December 31st and bring your accounting sheets up to date as soon after January 1st as you can. While federal taxes are usually not due until April 15th, you state's sales taxes may be due to the comptroller in late January. Your CPA will thank you for not waiting until the last minute.

# Chapter 15
# Selling The Business

Any number of reasons may get you thinking about selling the business.

"Things happen," is an often overused phrase, but it is correct, "things happen." In my case I had created a successful business that needed to be expanded and I was needing more space desperately. I could see multiple ways to increase business, to add employees and to really make the business grow. If I bought a larger building, all of my efforts would be needed to recoup the cost, handling more orders and hiring more employees.

The business was a blessing that had allowed me flexible time to do what I needed to do and still enjoy a nice income. Now my situation had changed and I had a choice between expanding the business or selling. At this point I was needing more time for family and since I wanted the business to continue to grow, I knew it was time to sell.

This decision did not come lightly. I had been thinking about it for over a year.

The company was well established, a proven winner and a very sellable asset. I was very proud of this accomplishment. The hard part was finding someone who would feel the same way as I did about the business. As silly as it may seem, when you create a business, nurture and develop it, it becomes almost as important as one of your children.

Different circumstances may get you to thinking about selling your business. Burnout may be a factor. When the business is no longer fun, you should focus on an exit strategy. The business will always be work but when it becomes work that you don't look forward to, your attitude will affect the business.

Make an appointment with an attorney to talk about your business and your intentions to sell. The initial consultation is usually free but be sure to ask before making the appointment. Don't wait until the last minute to hire an attorney. They can give you valuable information as to what to expect, how much to ask, what the buyer may want, your responsibilities to the buyer now and in the future and their fee for handling the details of the sale. This information will be useful in the negotiation stage and you will know how much to increase the asking price to recover the attorney's fees, legal filing fees, etc.

There are a couple of ways to sell your business. You can sell it intact with all of the inventory, equipment, website and domain name. If the business is growing and has a great reputation and loyal customers, this way will be more valuable to you. You will be selling things that you can't touch - intangibles like the reputation of the business. The promise not to compete with the new owner for a stated time period will be worth something to the new owner as well.

Your attorney should check a buyer's financial credit history prior to revealing any details of the company or producing any financial statements. You want to be sure they can pay your asking price. They should also sign a non-disclosure agreement which your attorney can provide.

As you negotiate the sales price, your data bases will show the prospective buyer the type of customer that has been buying from you and will suggest future marketing potential. Your last 3 - 5 year's IRS tax returns will also show the sales each year and the past growth of the company. Your customer data base and your sales growth rate will be key to getting a good sales price.

Any awards or special mentions on local TV or in magazines will also be an important factor in determining a sales price. This type of exposure carries over in the business and the new owner will be allowed to capitalize on the accolades you have received.

Set a price for your company and if you are firm on the price, let any prospective buyer know that up front. If you are willing to take offers, don't be offended at a low first offer. The buyer wants to see if you can afford to wait for a better offer or if you need to sell immediately and will take less.

If a prospective buyer makes a statement like "it is not worth more than what I am offering," just smile and thank them but tell them that you do not want to sell at that price at this time. You will get some ugly people making snide remarks about the worth of your business. Even though it is hard, try not to take it personally. Some people want something for nothing and these people usually will not negotiate fairly. These people are not good candidates to purchase your business. It is best to end the conversation and go on to the next prospect.

The first time I offered my business for sale, a gentleman offered me 25% of the wholesale cost of the inventory only and nothing more. He claimed that he bought and sold businesses all the time and mine wasn't worth any more than that. I was hurt, mad and disgusted. I was trying to sell a thriving business, not have a fire sale! I told him thanks but no thanks and took it off the market. A year later I offered the business for sale again. This time I found a buyer who saw value in the business and in its future potential. We negotiated a sale price that I was happy with and so was the new owner.

In the negotiations, point out the positive things about your business, its earnings and growth rate. Never promise a buyer that they can do as well as you or better. You never know what may happen when they take over the business and if they feel you promised any type of future earnings that they did not experience, may decide to take you to court.

If you are not interested in having the business continue, or you want to reserve the business name for yourself, you may choose to sell only the inventory and equipment and close up shop.

If it is an inventory only sale, most buyers will not want to give you what the items are actually worth. You may be in a situation where something is better than nothing but try to get the true wholesale value back. Someone just starting out in the business may prefer to purchase your inventory and equipment so they can make a name for themselves.

The buyer may be willing to pay you more for your inventory and equipment if they are being trained. Offer the buyer your time as an incentive, teaching them how to create the baskets and consulting on other business details.

So how do you find a buyer? A couple of options for you to consider:

<u>Family, Friends or Employees</u> - If you have employees, friends or family members working in the business, these may be the first people to approach about buying your business. If selling to a family member or a friend, they may expect you to "give them the store" so this option may not be right for you.

Craig's List - www.craigslist.com. Advertising is free so describe it well, include lots of pictures and set your asking price. Don't include the company name or phone number. You don't want everyone knowing that the business is for sale while you are operating.

Craig's List will assign an e-mail to your ad for people to contact you. You can then pick and choose which individuals you would like to contact.

I sold my business through Craig's List and I was contacted by people who wanted me to finance, who told me they did not have any money but they wanted my business and other interesting offers - all of which I chose not to respond to the e-mails!

Ebay - www.ebay.com. There is a listing fee to put your business on Ebay, even if you do not sell. A percentage of the sale price is also charged if you find a buyer and complete the sale. The sale is in auction form. Set a minimum acceptable price so if the bids don't meet what you are willing to take, you don't have to sell. If you don't set this minimum, the sale amount will be the amount of the highest bid.

I listed my business on Ebay with a minimum and I was glad that I did because the highest bid was ridiculous. I was trying to sell a viable business, not have a going out of business fire sale! This avenue did not work for us but it may work better for you.

Business Brokers - Some brokers will not be interested in your business if it does not include real estate or if you do not have an actual "brick and mortar" storefront. Brokers are beginning to realize there are thriving home-based and internet businesses. Search until you find one that specializes in these businesses.

Business brokers generally charge a percentage of the selling price. If you use a business broker, be sure that they have the proper license in your state to sell real estate, if any is involved. Likewise, if you have real estate and you are selling through a real estate broker, are they qualified to sell the business assets and intangibles or just the real estate? Get the answers prior to committing to any contract and agreeing to any fees. Usually all commission sales percentages are subject to negotiation so get the best deal you can. Ask if the broker's commission will cover all closing costs and attorney's fees or will these be in addition to their commission?

As e-commerce and home-based businesses become more prevalent, business brokers will be more receptive. If you don't want to handle the sale and marketing details of your business, a business broker may be a good fit for you.

The Value of The Business - In talking to business brokers I did gain some valuable information. There are numerous ways to evaluate a business but the value of the inventory is usually at wholesale cost. The price of used equipment is market value or remaining depreciable value.

The value of things like 1) good will, 2) your customer base, 3) your good name, 4) your position on Google and the other search engines, 5) your company's good reputation, 6) if the business is old enough to have a recognizable name in the industry, 7) how much is it worth to the new owner to have you not to enter the same industry for 3 - 5 years (no compete agreement), is wide open.

Here are a couple of methods of estimating the value of your business:

1) The business could be worth 1/2 of the gross sales from last year plus the inventory at cost and the value of the equipment.

2) If you have an excellent standing with the search engines, your company can be worth up to 8 - 10 times your net profit from last year.

These two methods are only a guideline because the value of anything is what a buyer is willing to give and a seller is willing to take. You can say something is worth a million dollars but unless you find a buyer that is willing to pay that million dollars, is it really worth that much?

Attorney - Once you find a buyer and agree on a sales price, have your attorney draw up any necessary paperwork. This is one time you do not want to scrimp, you want the sale to be perfectly legal. Hire an attorney who is very familiar with and has closed several business sales - it does make a difference.

The buyer may also have an attorney but it is in your best interest to have the paperwork drawn up by your attorney. Your attorney will have your best interests at heart and in some aspects of the paperwork, such as the no-compete clause, they can design it more in your favor. The buyer should be given the opportunity to have their attorney review all of the paperwork at their expense.

Who will provide the attorney to draw up the legal papers, and who will pay the attorney, should be part of the discussion with your buyer.

Financing - When you find a buyer, don't finance the sale of your business. You may be able to sell quicker and for more money if you carry a note, and even collect interest in the interim, but why would you want to if the bank won't? If the prospective buyer can not get the full amount from his bank you should not finance the remaining balance either. This may sound harsh but if you are still invested in the business you will want to have a say in how it is run, especially when the new owner seems to be messing things up.

What if the new owner runs your beautiful company in the ground, leaving you with a worthless promissory note and a destroyed asset? You will have to go back to work and rebuild your reputation before trying to sell it again. If you truly want to sell, don't finance it, get full payment and move on.

After the sale - After you sell the business you will visit the company website. You will see changes and wonder "why are they doing it that way?" or think "that won't work." The new owner has paid for the privilege to make mistakes just like you did. Make the sale, let go and allow yourself to move on.

When you sell a business you are generally asked to sign a "no-compete contract." This is to assure the new owner you won't sell the business and then start a new company that directly competes with the one they just bought. After all, you would be their greatest competition!

Depending on how the contract is written, you can use your experiences to teach others or take a long deserved rest. Entrepreneurs like yourself don't stay still for very long. The wheels in your head will start to spin. You may look at a product and decide how to make it better or get upset with the customer service in a certain industry and vow to correct it. Entrepreneurs are always thinking, looking ahead to that next great challenging adventure.

# Chapter 16

## Special Forms You Need

### 1. Telephone / Custom Order Form

This is a 'must have.' If you are like me, when the business phone rings you grab the closest note pad. You will be talking to your customer and forget to ask something important, like "what should the gift card to say?" or the expiration date of their credit card. It is a little embarrassing to have to call the customer back.

This form will keep everything in order and remind you of things you need to ask. When taking a phone order, follow it top to bottom. Read back all of the information to the person placing the order. Spell each name to be sure you have them right. Verify the "send to" and "bill to" addresses, make sure you have any apartment or suite numbers (very important and often missed by the caller), as well as the credit card number and information. Do this on every order and don't assume you have it right.

Make only a couple of copies because after using the form a time or two you may see things that should be changed for your particular business. Make any adjustments needed and then print several copies to leave next to the telephone.

Some of the items are for your use only to fill out later, such as wholesale basket cost and service charges. This information will help you spot rising costs and help you adjust your retail basket costs if necessary.

Invoice numbers will be assigned by your shopping cart, but you will need a custom order number system also. We used a date system followed by the number of the order for that day - for example: 20130501-1, 20130501-2, etc.

On custom orders, list the items included in the basket on the back of the order form and figure your retail amount. A customer ordering a custom basket will usually give you a dollar amount that they want to spend. Be sure to clarify if this is the total they want to spend, or is it just for the basket and then you can add the shipping charge. Usually it is the total amount for the gift and shipping combined.

When you send out a custom or phone order, send the customer an invoice copy with a receipt for their credit card charge. This is not necessary on orders that come through the website, unless a customer calls and changes an order or wants to add expedited shipping. In this case print out the online order, mark any changes needed, assign a new custom order number and create a new invoice. Send the customer a detailed invoice copy and a credit card receipt. Attach this custom order form to your invoice copy and file with today's orders. Write the date on the invoice you mailed the customer's receipt for your records.

**<u>Order Worksheet - August 2013</u>**        Invoice #_____

Date:_____        <u>Bill To:</u>_____

Requested Delivery Date:_____        Who Placed the order?_____

Is this a surprise?    Yes    No        Company:_____

<u>Deliver To:</u>        Address:_____

Name:_____        City:_____

Street Address:_____        State:_____Zip:_____

City:_____        Telephone:_____

State:_____Zip:_____        Alt. Phone:_____

Telephone:_____        E-Mail:_____

Business Address   /   Residential Address


Custom Basket - Price agreed to $_____

Retail Price - Custom Basket $_____

Shipping Charges $_____

Sales Tax @_____% $_____

Total Custom Sale: $_____


Website Basket - Which One? _____

Basket Cost  $_____

Additions or Substitutions  $_____

Shipping Charges        $_____

Sales Tax @_____% $_____

Total Sale  $_____


Visa    Master Card    American Express      Exp. Date:_____/_____ CCV#_____

Credit Card Number:_____

C/C Approval Code:_____

Name on the Card:_____

Is the billing address the same as the credit card mailing address?     Yes     No

If not, the Credit Card billing address:_____

_____

Special instructions:_____

_____

Words for the gift card:_____

_____

_____

_____

Signed: (Love, Mom, etc)_____


Marketing Information - How did you hear about us?

Internet Search  /  Website  /  Referral  /  Postcard  /  Ad / _____

# 2. Wholesale Product Price Sheet

Use this sheet to calculate a custom basket price or when designing a new basket for the website.

If you quote an incorrect amount, don't go back to the customer and request more money. They will expect you to deliver at the price you promised. If you misquote a basket price, take the loss and deliver as promised, then use the sheet next time.

The form can be kept in a word processing document or in a data base, which ever you are more comfortable using. Updated the form with any changes immediately.

The containers, their sizes and prices should be listed first. Then products should be listed by vendor in alphabetical order. The prices should be your wholesale cost.

If you have 'add on' items like books, paperweights, mugs or bowls, these should be at the end of the form. Keep a copy near the telephone with your custom order form. When there is a wholesale price change, or you add a new product or supplier, update the sheet, date it and print it out. This list can also make your monthly inventory and reordering a little easier.

Product Price Sheet Example:

## **Wholesale Product Prices - August 10, 2013   ( last update )**

Containers:

| | | |
|---|---|---|
| 8" Round  3.50 | 10" Round    4.50 | 12" Round    5.50 |
| 15" Texas  7.50 | 18" Texas    10.50 | 22" Texas    14.50 |
| Market basket - 1/4 peck    2.00 | 1/2 peck    2.00 | |

### Angor Chili

Chili Mix    4.50          Bean Seasoning    4.50

### Jimmy O's

Spicy Rub    3.00          Liquid Smoke Marinade    6.00

Lemon Pepper Rub  3.00          Hot Sauce  3.00

### Coffee City

Any flavor coffee    1.00          Any flavor tea    1.00

### MCM Cocoa

Cocoa Mix    4.00

### Oliver Pecans

Chocolate pecans - 8 oz - 8.00          4 oz - 5.00

Any other flavor - 8 oz - 3.50          4 oz - 2.50

### Morrison's

Pancake mix   1.00          Cornbread mix    1.00          Gravy mix    1.00

### Extras

Texas trivia book -    5.95          Cookbook - 6.25          Mug or Bowl - 15.00

# 3. Supplier List And Notes

Another sheet that will come in handy is your supplier list. If you need to order supplies in a hurry, you won't have time to drag out your catalogs. Add a little notation about what you buy from them or their trade name.

Are there any special discounts that you have to ask for? Make any discount notes on your supplier list. Some companies give a discount for immediate payment. One of our vendors would deduct 5% off my order if I paid by check instead of using a credit card.

Note on the supplier list how long it takes for orders to be shipped. Does the vendor produce the product when you order or do they keep an inventory? Do they only make candy on Mondays and ship out on Wednesdays? Some smaller companies concentrate on production on certain days and do not ship on those days. Note this on your list. You may need to locate another vendor for this product to fill in any gaps while you wait on your favorite supplier and their schedule.

Your list will help at Christmas as a reminder so you won't forget to order from any of your suppliers. Make a copy of your list and go right down the line. Make notes of what you need, call the vendors to order and check them off as you go. It is sheer panic when you realize you forgot the chocolate pecans everybody loves, and it is easy to forget an item that you only order at Christmas.

If you deal with any manufacturer's reps, after their information list the actual company names. Add any notes that may help you along the way. This list can be in alphabetical order or in the order of importance to you.

Here is an example to use when making your own:

## Supplier / Vendor List  August 10, 2013

Gourmet Products, Inc.  Ann  800-541-2215

   PO Box 2590, Jupiter, FL  33468-2590

  Vinetique - Baskets and trays - usually 1 day shipping

  Pecans International - flavored pecans and jelly beans

  The Great Texas Line Press - small trivia books and cowboy cookbooks


The Chili House  Patty  800-821-2462

   PO Box 1204, Marshall, TX  75671

  Chili Mix - Pinto Bean Seasoning - Meat Seasoning


Jimmy O's  Jimmy  888-282-2216

  PO Box 359, Bergheim, TX  78004

Dry rubs, barbeque sauce, hot sauce, liquid marinades - usually 1 day shipping.  Keeps most items in stock.

# 4. Purchase Order Form

Use this form when ordering your supplies. It is for your use and not to send to suppliers. It is a reminder of what you ordered and when. Keep all of your pending orders together in a file on your desk until the order arrives. If you don't receive the order in a couple of days, you know to check with the supplier.

Make written notes concerning the order on this form. Did you order by phone? Who did you speak to and the time? What is the promised ship out date and expected arrival date? Mark the date of the order and its estimated arrival date on the purchase order and your desk calendar.

If you order by fax or e-mail, always call and confirm the company received the order. Some faxes and e-mails seem to go to 'cyber heaven.' Note the customer service reps name you spoke with, the date and time.

The manufacturer will not know the exact shipping costs until your order is packaged and ready to go. Have them call you back with an exact final order total. An invoice should be with your order when it arrives, if it isn't call and request one.

Once the order arrives, check the condition of each item and count everything. No matter how busy you are, count the incoming inventory prior to putting it on the shelf. When you are busy you may be tempted to put it on the shelf, but once it is mixed with your current stock, you may not realize what you had and what just came in. Count everything and check your purchase order before mixing any new stock with old stock.

Match your purchase order with what you received. Your order form should then be matched to the invoice to verify that you received what you were charged for. Check the invoice to be sure the prices are what you agreed to and then you can put the stock away. If there are any price changes, this is a good time to correct your wholesale product price sheet.

Attach your purchase order form to the invoice, list the product cost and incoming freight on your bookkeeping ledger and file the invoice with your other completed orders. The last invoice received should go on the top of the group, secured with a clip to keep them neat.

Make a copy of the invoice for the vendor's file and a second copy to attach to your credit card statement, if this is how the order was paid.

**A blank purchase order needs the following information:**

| Company Name | Order Date | Estimated Ship date |
|---|---|---|

| Product | Size | Quantity | Each price | Extended price |
|---|---|---|---|---|

Total   $_____

Freight   $_____

**A completed purchase order will look something like this:**

| Company Name | Order Date | Estimated Ship date |
|---|---|---|
| Jimmy O's | August 10, 2013 | will send out today |

| Product | Size | Quantity | Each price | Extended price |
|---|---|---|---|---|
| Spicy Rub | 7 oz | 12 | 6.00 | 72.00 |
| Peach Marinade | 12 oz | 12 | 6.00 | 72.00 |

Total   $   144.00

Freight   $_____

Total Charged   $_____

Jimmy - 10:00   8/10/13 - in stock and will ship today - should arrive tomorrow

Paid with American Express

# 5. Basket Information Sheet

This little "cheat sheet" was my life saver. I kept one in the office, one next to the telephone and two at the basket assembly workstation. Once you have created several baskets, you will automatically know what goes in a particular basket, but when a customer orders a basket that you haven't made in a while, this sheet lets you know exactly what goes in that particular basket. Especially usefully when you have 15 - 20 different baskets on your website.

I have had customers call and want the XYZ basket but with substitutions or additions. This form, along with my wholesale product price sheet, saves the day. When you are doing baskets as fast as you can at Christmas, this form keeps you focused and simplifies the assembly process.

In alphabetical order list the basket name, retail cost, the box size and the finished basket weight. Since UPS rounds everything off to the next pound this is a good way to save time, but always verify the weight of your boxes for the shipping label. This noted weight also comes in handy when figuring expedited shipping for a customer without having to actually create the basket.

List the type of basket or container and its size first, then the contents of each basket. Use shorthand if you want as long as you understand your notes. For example, 12" SQ is obviously a 12 inch square tray, or TX would be for a Texas shaped basket. I would list candied jalapenos as just "jal" and "4 salsas" instead of listing all of the flavors.

Divide each item with a " / " making it easier to read at a glance. When you are in a hurry the list of products seem to run together. After the basket is assembled, check your list one more time before sealing the basket so nothing is forgotten.

If you are using a graduated shipping schedule, list your shipping charges at the bottom for quick reference.

## Basket Contents - August 2013

Texas Chocolate Lovers     $49.95         10#    14 X 14 X 10

10" TX / TX fudge / 6 cho. tamales / 1/2# cho. pecans / hot cho. mix / fudge in a jar

Texas Hearty Breakfast     $32.95         7#    14 X 14 X 10

8" Round / syrup / preserves / pancake mix / gravy mix / biscuit mix / 2 coffees

Texas Super Basket     $89.95         15#    16 X 16 X 10

12" SQ / 4 salsas / jal / chili / bean / 2 soups / 4 pralines / 2 coffees / 2 teas

UPS Ground Shipping - for each basket

| | |
|---|---|
| 0 - 45.00 | 8.95 |
| 45.01 - 75.00 | 11.95 |
| 75.01 - 100.00 | 14.95 |
| 100.01 - 150.00 | 17.95 |

# Index